THE SUBVERSIVE VEGETARIAN

Tactics, Information and Recipes for the Conversion of Meat Eaters

by

MICHAEL COX

with recipes by
DESDA CROCKETT

Illustrated by Clive Birch

THORSONS PUBLISHERS LIMITED
Wellingborough, Northamptonshire

First published 1979

ISBN 0 7225 0570 1

Typeset by Harper Phototypesetters, Northampton,
printed by Biddles Ltd., Guildford, Surrey
and bound by Weatherby Woolnough Ltd.,
Wellingborough, Northamptonshire.

CONTENTS

INTRODUCTION

In 1890, at a meeting held under the auspices of the West Ham Vegetarian Society, vegetarians and carnivores put their respective ideologies to the test. The occasion was reported with gusto by the *Cambridge Review* — no doubt with the carnivorous prejudices of its Varsity readers firmly in mind. 'The proceedings appear to have been of a rather mixed character,' said the *Review* humorously. 'A hymn was sung, the drum and fife band "performed a selection for the delectation of the assembly", and the chairman preached the benefits of vegetarianism.'

After an affecting offering from the children's choir came the main event: a tug of war between vegetarians and carnivores. There were three rounds. In the first, three vegetarians vanquished four carnivores; in the second, six carnivores managed to pull over four vegetarians; but in the last and spectacularly conclusive round, six carnivores were pulled right over the line by a squad of victorious vegetable eaters. 'The champions of "roast beef"', said the *Cambridge Review*, 'retired discomfited, sadder and, let us hope, wiser men.'

The tug of war, metaphorically speaking, is still going on today. On the one side are ranged the committed vegetarians, increasingly augmented and encouraged by nutritional, medical and economic facts. On the other are the equally committed carnivores, strong and sure in the realization that they are still numerically superior and that they have a long and sturdy weight of tradition to back them up. Trials of strength are one way of making a point: but there are others, more subtle and, perhaps, finally more productive.

There is nothing more calculated to stiffen a carnivore's resistance to a reform of his diet than the sight of a ranting, holier-than-thou vegetarian who sees life as a constant vigil against eating or drinking anything that he knows, or suspects, is either detrimental to his physical system or inimical to his ethics. The common complaint by meat eaters that vegetarians are dour killjoys also has a depressing basis in fact and the taunt 'If you don't smoke, drink or eat meat, what do you do?' is often justified. The dedicated carnivore has at least the positive virtue of enjoying his food (and how often do we hear the cry, 'Oh, I do enjoy my meat!'), and though the reasons for giving up the consumption of animal flesh are becoming increasingly irresistible, an unashamed satisfaction in putting away a pound of rump steak is on the whole preferable to the faddist who worries himself silly over every mouthful.

This book proposes a middle way for vegetarians and for those thinking about giving up meat. It also suggests more devious tactics for survival in a largely meat-orientated society than most radical vegetarians are prepared to accept. For them the full frontal, full steam ahead attack is the thing: abuse the enemy; show him for the unfeeling immoral wretch that he is.

There are other, and better, ways of cracking an egg — or converting a carnivore. The tactics and information outlined in this book are designed to give strength to harassed vegetarians as well as to provide a basis for gradually undermining the inherited prejudices of meat eaters among family and friends.

I have called the process the subversive way because its essence is to let out information gradually so that it slowly coalesces in your meat eater's mind until it eventually becomes part of *his* way of thinking. Soon it no longer becomes an affront to everything he believes in to be told that eating meat can be bad for his health; after a time, with regular, carefully orchestrated assaults on his prejudices and his inherited ignorance, he finally comes to believe that the views that have been subtly infiltrated into his brain are his own.

The dispelling of ignorance is perhaps the main tactic. The second is more basic: to prove that vegetarian eating can be just as satisfying as a meat-based diet in the most conclusive and effective way possible — by the regular substitution of meat and two veg meals by good vegetarian menus.

The book therefore falls into two main sections. The first deals generally with ways and means of persuading others to cut down the amount of meat that they eat, with some of the social perils of being a vegetarian, and with the necessary art of self-defence. The second consists of recipes designed to appeal to meat eaters and which are meant to be used as substitutes for meat-based meals.

The hope is that the regular use of these recipes will accustom carnivores to meatless meals and bring home to them what is for vegetarians the glaring truism that a vegetarian diet is every bit as satisfying and as nourishing as one based on dead animals.

Many carnivores, of course, are sympathetic to the ethical and nutritional ideals of vegetarianism but feel unable, for one reason or another, to undertake a totally meatless diet. Some feel that they 'need' meat, for their work, perhaps, or for their weekend sport, and no amount of propaganda will convince them that this primitive belief in the power of blood is a false one. Others, whose job involves travelling, may reasonably argue that their day to day routine prohibits total abstention from meat and that they must preserve a flexible approach to eating.

However, it should be possible to reduce the meat intake of such people by a subtle process of infiltration: if they can experience a meatless meal that leaves them feeling as replete and satisfied as a T-bone steak, then the way is clear for further erosions of their faith in the power of meat.

The subversive process, then, together with a programme of humorous 'needling', can be used by any member of the family who is already convinced of the benefits of vegetarianism. The end result may not be a total rejection of dead cows and pigs, but it should, at least, lead to an observable reduction in meat consumption, an advantage in every way — morally, nutritionally and economically.

If you are the lone vegetarian in your family, especially if you are also the cook, the subversive way is the only practical means of bringing about a satisfactory and workable compromise with your meat eaters. You may not be able to convert everyone in your family, but you should at least be able to show them that life does not lose its meaning entirely if the centrepiece of Sunday lunch is not the steaming carcase of a late cow. In time, even the most tenacious carnivore ought to be able to tuck in happily to half a dozen vegetarian meals a week and, just as happily, accept the reasons for doing so.

From time to time, of course, you will need to defend yourself against belligerent meat eaters and you will then need more than a beautiful and noble conviction. In the first place, you must never be afraid to abandon the traditional and rather insulting image of the typical vegetarian as a gentle doe-eyed creature, pale of face, limp of wrist and docile of manner. On those occasions when your meat eating fellows decide to give you a hard time, as they often do; when they taunt you and tempt you and try to make out that your views are anti-social and unnatural — then it is absolutely necessary to give as good as you get. A bloody nose is often more satisfying than preserving a supercilious silence. Don't be afraid of loud-mouthed carnivores: it's meat that makes them that way.

By following the guidelines given in this book, and by keeping yourself constantly and accurately informed, you will be better able to withstand such attacks and the frequent and often depressing social pressures of being the odd one out.

1. BEING A VEGETABLE

It happened gradually, almost without my knowing it. Over a period of about six months my meat consumption was drastically reduced, but painlessly and in the nicest possible way. Then one day I realized that I could not face the steaming Shepherd's Pie (hitherto an object of intense craving) that had been placed before me. My career as a carnivore was over.

I have always had what is called a 'fellow feeling' for animals. I get on well with them and even flatter myself that I have come close to understanding the devious mentality of a cat. But in spite of this I had given little thought to the anomaly of combining a love of four-footed creatures with the regular practice of consigning certain of them to the fate of being dissolved by my gastric juices.

Even when I finally gave up meat and bade farewell forever to Shepherd's Pies and crispy bacon I gave little thought to the ethical reasons with which I *could* have justified my renunciation. It is only now, something more than a year later, that I have become aware of the issues in their wider implications. Up until now, I blush to admit, the basis of my conviction and the means of my conversion were the result of sheer physical satisfaction: my stomach finally decided the matter by finding nothing to complain of, indeed much to praise, in the adoption of a vegetarian diet.

Little by Little
It is not this easy for everyone. Many experience classic withdrawal symptoms after giving up meat and some vegetarians retain particular longings for years. In my case, the smell of bacon cooking tempted me for some months, though its grip on me is now happily relaxed.

However, I was not self-motivated in my renunciation of meat and I cannot claim very much of the credit for it. As well as being morally sluggish in the matter of animal rights I was wheedled into vegetarianism by a subtle and determined *agent provocateur*. Little by little my traditional expectations of what constituted 'a good meal' were altered by simple but altogether unobtrusive means.

The only begetter of my subversion had no sinister motive and there was nothing underhand or unpleasantly covert about it all. The process consisted chiefly in substituting a non-meat meal for a meat meal and in the gentle but firm exposure of my ethical confusion over liking animals but continuing to eat them. I was not the only one to be converted: other members of the family went the same way, and as the success rate grew it seemed that the principle was a sound one.

Pressures
Now that I am a vegetarian, and now that people know that I am, there are problems. In some cases I have become an object of curiosity, some weird species of animal who walks around in a cage of my own devising. In others, I experience a certain degree of hostility. Saying, 'Oh, no thank you. I'm a vegetarian', sparks off an array of reactions, from glassy, uncomprehending stares to undisguised and definitely unfriendly guffaws. It is not enough to *be* a vegetarian: you have to acquire the ability to justify your anti-social habits to the carnivorous majority.

The psychological pressures on new vegetarians are considerable and too little recognized. Instead of already committed vegetarians blithely preaching their gospel to potential converts they should make sure the new disciples know exactly what they are letting themselves in for. It takes time and determination to accustom yourself to the fact that you are no longer in the majority. From the moment you give up meat the world becomes a different place. You can no longer eat where you please; doors previously open are now firmly closed to you. Any sort of journey away from home is a major undertaking as far as obtaining suitable food is concerned, and on top of the practical difficulties are the thousand and one little annoyances and adjustments you are forced to come to terms with.

The regular socializer, of course, bears the brunt of all this; but for all of us there are hurdles to be crossed. Let us take one possible scenario.

The Dinner and Dance
The car has been parked. You walk up the steps, past two neatly

boxed bay trees, and you shiver slightly as the night air infiltrates the rather feeble protection afforded by your evening shirt, wishing, as you nod benignly to people, that social conventions allowed you to wear an evening pullover as well. But still, things will soon warm up. A few drinks and a couple of foxtrots and the cold night air will be forgotten in a bright haze of small talk, slightly out of tune saxophones, and perspiring foreheads.

Your wife disappears to powder something or other. You stand, grinning sociably, in the lobby, a feeling of faint misgiving in the pit of your stomach. Annual Dinner and Dances can be trying occasions for the best of us, but for some it fairly bristles with problems; for, if you are a certain class of person, one half of the evening's delights presents a formidable problem: if, that is, you are unfortunate enough to be a vegetarian amidst an army of carnivores.

Dinner is served. You hope that the social secretary has not forgotten that you do not eat meat (you did go to great trouble to make him fully aware of the fact) and that he has laid on, as he promised, 'something special'.

You sit down. The first course arrives and your spirits rise. Instead of the Brown Windsor everyone else is getting the waitress places before you a dish of what looks remarkably like vegetable soup — a pale, golden-coloured liquid supporting what seem to be carrots, peas, tinned tomatoes and various other vegetable-like objects. Better just make sure, though. Your sensitive, well-trained nose hovers just above the shimmering liquid and then suddenly recoils with a horrified twitch: chicken stock. You might have known.

A hurried whisper to the waitress confirms your suspicions, produces a strange look, and extracts a mumbled promise that she will speak to someone about it. The main course arrives and you find yourself confronted with some atrophied lettuce and a few more pieces of geriatric saladings, all of which serve as a rather seedy backcloth to a moist-looking rectangle of cheese that continues to perspire freely as you gaze at it. And so you grit your teeth and consume your non-flesh repast as placidly as you can while all around you is a riot of meat and gravy.

The Odd One Out
Once again you are the odd one out, and it can be a dispiriting experience. You are constantly being cheered by reports that more and more people are giving up meat, but somehow the ratio of

carnivores to vegetarians seems to remain static and things in general don't seem to change. It's still just as hard to get a decent non-meat meal away from home — in a motorway service area, for instance (assuming that a decent meal of any sort exists in such places). And a touring holiday can deteriorate into a depressing ritual of cheese sandwiches and salads, or, if your creed allows, the occasional treat of fish and chips.

Not that people do not try and accommodate you from time to time: they do. But even when they become aware of your quirk and attempt to satisfy it, their powers of invention are often unable to keep pace with their willingness to oblige you. Having to face a cheese salad for the third time in four days in a lonely Scottish hotel can begin to shake the ideological foundations of the most committed.

It's the easiest thing in the world, on the other hand, to be a carnivore. You don't even have to try. Society, as it now stands, is made for you. No one thinks you are odd because you make a habit of eating the burnt corpses of animals. You can go anywhere and be reasonably sure that you will be able to get what, in your book, is a good meal, and there are not many places where you cannot sink your fork and your teeth into the underdone buttocks of a late cow, or titillate your palate with slices hacked off a once frisky lamb.

The Vegetarian's Lot
But if your gorge rises at the thought of eating dead and decomposing flesh you will find that you hold a very weak hand indeed in the eating away from home game. You have to become philosophical, in the broadest sense, ready to accept the unacceptable in order to hang on to your convictions and keep yourself alive. When I still ate meat I sat next to a vegetarian at dinner in a Cardiff hotel. There was nothing on the menu that the poor chap could have, and so he asked if he could just have some cheese with the main course vegetables. This he duly got — covered with gravy.

I felt then, as I feel now, that you have to be brave (some would say foolish) as well as resourceful to be a vegetarian, especially if you spend much time away from home. The situation is changing and things are improving. But it can still be very difficult. Becoming a vegetarian — 'being a vegetable' — is still, in spite of everything, to become part of a minority.

The Ubiquitous Egg
What would we do without eggs? For many moderate vegetarians

it is often — all too often — a life saver. In restaurants, when we shyly announce that we do not eat meat, the alternative offered to us is invariably an omelette — a worthy object in itself, but disastrously prone to overkill by unimaginative or uninterested restauranteurs. The omelette, of course, can be made into quite an appealing dish: it is certainly a delicious light lunch. But it has its limitations.

As far as most caterers are concerned, meatless cookery resolves itself into two basic alternatives: omelettes or cheese salads. The orthodox catering trade in general seems blissfully unaware of the revolution in non-meat cuisine that has taken place over the last few years.

> When I 'phoned a super-duper top-class *haute cuisine* restaurant . . . for a reservation, the ex-military owner flatly refused to prepare a special vegetarian dinner, even though, on this occasion, he could have charged me the earth. He had this explanation: 'One doesn't go to one's shirt-maker to buy a suit.' Meatless cookery, in other words, is no concern of the carnivores.[1]

Privations, then, are part and parcel of the vegetarian way of life. More than most people, even in an age of generally declining standards, vegetarians must often steel themselves to making do. Very often it's that or going hungry.

'Out, damned spot!'

Byron, in *Don Juan,* made the connection between the English fondness for meat and their warlike disposition — between, as he put it, 'beef' and 'battle'. Carnivores today, reacting purely on inherited prejudice, still make a similar if unconscious connection. For them, a person who does not eat meat is taking a dangerous line. They believe that the vegetarian is denying his body something vital, something inescapably essential. This is a fallacy (see Chapter Two), but the feeling is part of a primitive reflex, a residual, implicit belief in the power of blood.

To some extent we all share this belief since it is ingrained in us — an instinct peculiar to the species. From the dawn of human consciousness men associated blood with life and the cessation of its function with the extinction of life. As it flowed from the body, so life itself ebbed away. This identification of blood with the life force deepened until blood became a symbol of the soul, a stream that carried with it the spiritual as well as the physical nature of Man.

From this association of blood and being arose the taboos on certain foods — such as the prohibition against eating the flesh of certain animals by the Jews. These taboos were based on the belief that to take in the blood of an animal was, in some sense, to absorb its nature.

Other societies, however, took a different view based on the same logic. They saw blood as a source of power. To drink the blood of a powerful enemy (or, as the Masai warriors did, to drink the blood of lions) was to assimilate his strength; similarly, to eat his brains, as the headhunters of Borneo did, was to take advantage of his mental powers and make them one's own.

All this has had a peculiar and little discussed consequence for vegetarians, because the ultimate version of this primitive logic is enshrined in the Christian Communion service. There have been more obvious consequences, too. With these beliefs imprinted on our collective unconscious it is easy to understand the fears that meat eaters feel at the prospect of giving up what they consider to be a source of essential strength. Behind their fears is a vast web of associations, superstitions and cultural attitudes.

Soya Protein

The concept of blood as the river of life continues to exert a powerful psychological hold even today. It is a force that no vegetarian should underestimate. It surely underlies the general disinclination of the average housewife to provide her family with soya protein instead of chunks of stewing steak: no amount of arguing about the nutritional sufficiency of soya products, it seems, can overcome this residual unconscious belief in blood.

This is, perhaps, why the great soya revolution has not materialized, even though Rank Hovis McDougall and other giant food producers have put money as well as faith behind soya products. It might seem that hard-headed corporations like R.H.M. would not waste time and money on soya protein unless they were entirely convinced that there was a future in them, and they have certainly remained confidently aloof from the strenuous opposition of cattle farmers and from the continuing indifference of the public.

But at the moment, more textured soya protein is sold in pet foods in Britain than in food for human consumption. The reason, according to Mr Bill Pringle, Technical Director of The British Arkady Company, is that 'You do not have to educate dogs, except by giving them the stuff.'[2]

Exactly. Dogs do not need to be convinced intellectually of the value and benefits of soya protein; nor, more importantly, do their unconscious minds respond to the archetypal impulses that prompt many housewives and consumers in general to turn away from soya protein in favour of food that is rich with the red stream of life.

The Shadow of Dracula

Vegetarians, therefore, are people who have somehow conquered this mythopoeic belief in the regenerative power of blood. This abnormality of theirs, for that is what it is, accounts for the sense of apartness that many vegetarians experience. It is, after all, an extreme step to place oneself voluntarily outside the circle of ingrained beliefs and assumptions within which most of the tribe live. Little wonder that people look upon you with amazement, incredulity or hostility: in essence, the vegetarian has become a renegade — figuratively, and often literally, an outsider.

I do not think that the power of these primitive, ingrained beliefs in blood has been fully taken into account in the great dietary debate. It is, to my mind, a substantial barrier to those who would wish to make this a vegetarian world. Think for a moment of that imposing and resonant figure, Dracula:

> The vampire bites his victims; and anyone with the slightest knowledge of Freud knows that a bite is a sado-erotic kiss; in *Dracula* the female vampires around Jonathan Harker's bed comment that his health and strength mean 'kisses for us all' . . . Blood is profoundly involved with sexuality in man's psyche . . . And modern psychology has shown the predominance of blood and blood-letting in the erotic fantasies of many psychiatric patients.[3]

With all these potent images and associations ranged against him it is little wonder that the vegetarian occasionally begins to wilt under the enormous psychological pressures that society's collective unconscious is capable of applying. All this is worth remembering next time you are locked in argumentative combat with a meat eater and feel that you are getting the worst of it.

Blood is the very stuff of life and meat partakes of its qualities and of its mythical and psychological associations. Sometimes no amount of factual evidence or moral exhortations can conquer this primordial logic. There is then nothing left but to give in gracefully and enjoy your nut rissole.

Babes and Sucklings

Espousing the vegetarian cause as a thinking mature adult is one thing: taking the decision to give up meat on behalf of an unborn child is quite another.

If you are a newly-converted vegetarian mother-to-be you will have quite legitimate worries about the sufficiency of your diet for your baby. The straight answer to the question, 'Is a vegetarian diet safe for pregnant women *and* their babies?, is 'Yes' — that is, if you take certain fundamental precautions.

In fact there are specific advantages in a vegetarian diet, if it is properly and sensibly balanced. For one thing, you will tend to get the required amount of folic acid, a vitamin that is 50 to 90 per cent destroyed by cooking, since vegetarians are more likely to eat the raw fruits and vegetables that supply folic acid. Fibre, too, is generally more plentiful in a vegetarian diet and this is especially important during pregnancy when food moves more slowly through the digestive tract.

Finally, vegetarians are on the whole more 'health conscious' than non-vegetarians and are less likely to load themselves with empty calorie-laden foods, and pregnancy is a time when every mouthful should count nutritionally.

However, and this cannot be stressed too much, care is needed. You should make sure that you obtain the following specific nutrients in the correct amounts: protein, calcium, iron, vitamin B12, vitamin B, vitamin C, vitamin B6 (riboflavin), and vitamin D. Make sure your diet is well balanced *before* pregnancy; do not diet or fast during pregnancy; take sensible exercise, and take vitamin and mineral supplements if so advised. Above all, seek expert medical and nutritional advice from the start or if you are at all worried that your diet is insufficient. The Vegetarian Society have a helpful leaflet, 'Vegetarian Infant Feeding' for when the baby is born.

These are the essential practical measures every vegetarian mother should take. Whether she should impose her beliefs on a developing foetus or a growing child who has no say in the matter is too large and complex a question to be dealt with here. The dangers of a strict ideology, however, are too great not to be considered, if only briefly. They were given wide prominence in 1979 by a report in the *British Medical Journal* by four doctors. The report was provocatively titled: 'Malnutrition in Infants Receiving Cult Diets: A Form of Child Abuse'. Their summary was as follows:

Severe nutritional disorders, including kwashiorkor, marasmus, and rickets, were seen in four children and were due to parental food faddism, which should perhaps be regarded as a form of child abuse. All disorders were corrected with more normal diets and vitamin supplements.

In view of the potentially serious consequences of restricted diets being fed to children, families at risk should be identified and acceptable nutritional advice given. When children are found to be suffering from undernutrition due to personal food faddism a court order will normally be a necessary step in providing adequate treatment and supervision.[4]

The parents involved in the four case reports were extremists in dietary matters, to say the least. In the first case the parents were converts to a cult whose main tenet was an adherence to an extremely restricted, uncooked vegetable diet and the child had received only breast milk and uncooked fruit and vegetables. In the second case the father was a vegetarian and the mother followed a macrobiotic diet. At the age of four weeks their baby was started on a macrobiotic infant food called kokoh, which is made of rice, oats, wheat, beans and sesame flour. It was totally insufficient for the needs of a growing baby. The four parents in the final two cases all followed a macrobiotic diet.

The issues raised by this report are undeniably serious and the problem it has identified needs close and constant scrutiny in the future. But, inevitably, the excessive ideological zeal of these faddists (and in these cases they clearly deserve the term) has been extended by the media to cover all those who follow a non-meat diet. In fact, of course, the 'abuses' of which the *B.M.J.* report speaks cannot, with justice, be applied to the way moderate, sensible vegetarians bring up their children — and moderate, sensible vegetarians form the majority of non-meat eaters.

The dangers, certainly are there, but care, common sense and the constant seeking of advice should ensure that babies brought up on a non-meat diet are every bit as healthy, if not healthier, than those who grow up with the taste of blood in their mouths.

Being a vegetable, then, as we have come facetiously to call our vegetarian lifestyle, bristles with problems. In no sense is it a soft option and anyone who has the temerity to go against the grain must be prepared for all manner of inconveniences, frustrations and worries.

Is it all worth it? That is a question each vegetarian must answer for himself. This book assumes that the decision has now been taken and that you are prepared to face the consequences. The first step in the survival game and a necessary preliminary to the subversive process is to take a few lessons in the art of self-defence.

1. Roger Elliot, *Alive*, June 1978.
2. Quoted in *The Times*, 24 November 1978.
3. Douglas Hill, *Man, Myth and Magic*, p. 2928.
4. *B.M.J.*, 1979, 1, 296-298.

2. LOOKING AFTER YOURSELF

It soon becomes obvious to the fledgling vegetarian that the arguments against his new eating habits invariably resolve themselves into a neat pile of hoary old chestnuts. Out they come, time and again: the same old myths, the same old objections — and the inevitable misconceptions. This chapter briefly describes a few of the most common arguments against a vegetarian diet, for, conversion being a two-way process, you will often be confronted by questions which, if you are not prepared for them, can seriously hamper your chances of convincing your questioner of the justice of your cause.

The Wider View

Malnutrition is not confined to the underdeveloped Third World countries. It is one of the greatest ironies of our time that in America, the apotheosis of 'development', where hardly anyone actually starves, the danger of undernourishment, of malnutrition in a strict sense, is high. Though North Americans consume vast quantities of edible substances, what those substances actually provide in nutritional terms is, at best, adequate; at worst, positively dangerous.

The same patterns of eating are in evidence in Britain: too much is consumed of what gives, in nutritional benefits, too little. Taste, meaning what pleases us, and convenience take precedence over what is good for us; indeed being told that something is 'good for us' invokes adverse psychological reactions: we have all been made to eat things we don't like by this same exhortation.

But there is a breaking point, in a personal as well as a historical sense. Medical evidence of diet-linked diseases, from cancer to heart failure, is now overwhelming and is becoming apparent to more and more people. Inadequate dietary patterns combined with life styles that do little or nothing to keep the physical system up to scratch have led to a deadly harvest of disease and debility and it is now a matter of individual and social concern that Western society looks long and hard at the way it eats and at the prospects before it if substantial changes are not made.

Ignorance

Ignorance about what we eat is a fact of life. It goes hand in hand with a general ignorance of what actually goes on inside our bodies. Of course we do not actually need to think about the way our bodies miraculously continue to function day after day. We only become conscious of our internal mechanisms when they impinge on our consciousness, usually through pain; when, that is, we suspect a malfunction. Otherwise, the body's processes continue, whether we give a thought to them or not.

We cannot, though, remain totally aloof from the world within us. Every single day we are responsible for what goes on in that world in the simple matter of refuelling. Doing what is best for ourselves would seem the only logical and sensible course, but in fact most people give little thought to the vital question of what is best for them. They simply remain content to eat what pleases them.

Historically, Man learned by trial and error what things were good to eat and what was to be avoided, and we are the inheritors of centuries of accumulated wisdom. We know, for instance, that bread is good for us, being made from a grain that, since the earliest civilizations, has been established as a staple and nutritious food. But once we remove ourselves from a direct experience of the primary source, then our instinctual trust in the value of bread is misplaced and prompts us to consume some very strange creations indeed.

There have been tirades enough against the iniquities of white bread, but even though many supermarkets are now stocking bread that has not had all its essential fibre and natural goodness refined out of it many people, perhaps the majority, still think of bread in terms of thin, white, cellophane-wrapped slices.

Bread is just one example of how the food processing industry has driven a wedge between the consumer and natural products. The convenience foods that are eaten in such huge quantities are at one, perhaps two or three, removes from nature: just look around you at what people are putting into their baskets next time you are in a supermarket. In spite of all the campaigning and the proliferation of nutritional and medical information over the last few years the continuing preponderance of tins and packets of devitalized and denatured foods is still glaringly obvious. People still believe that because something is edible it is, by some occult process, sufficient for the body's needs. White bread is edible, but it is not nutritious; charcoal-broiled steaks are edible, but eating them regularly may be as dangerous as smoking.

The Question of Sufficiency

Meat is still at the centre of most people's dietary thinking: meals, to many people, are incomplete without a main course that has animal flesh as its basis. But while it is a good source of protein, meat has little else to offer. The moral objections to eating meat must always be worthy of respect, but the *practical* objections carry more immediate weight and their implications affect everyone, no matter what their moral stance on animal rights may be.

Modern meat-based eating habits do little to dispel the ignorance about what the body needs to sustain itself efficiently and healthily. If people had more basic knowledge about the workings of their own bodies the fear and mistrust of vegetarianism might be dispelled. The belief generally is that a vegetarian diet is necessarily deficient — a conclusion arrived at by the fact that something (meat) has been given up. Faced with someone who believes that giving up meat will involve them in some sort of risk, what can you say to reassure them?

You can state simply and confidently that it is a fact beyond dispute that a vegetarian diet (and, indeed, a vegan diet) can provide all the nutritional requirements necessary for healthy and efficient living. This is not to say that giving up meat automatically results in health and bounding vitality, but that its potential for doing so is great.

This is becoming less of a hopeful boast with the accumulation of medical and scientific evidence. For instance, at the Ninth Annual Conference of the U.K. Vegetarian Society, Dr J. Gear, of the Department of Social Medicine at Oxford, who had been closely involved with an epidemiological study of vegetarians in Oxford, spoke of research that had confirmed vegetarian claims that a non-meat diet was intrinsically more healthy. Dr Gear and his team had examined the incidence of dietary fibre in different groups and the relationship of fibre to asymptomatic diseases (that is, diseases that reveal no obvious symptoms), especially diverticulosis (inflammation of the colon).

'In the past', said Dr Gear, 'many enquiries have dwelt on the hazards of a vegetarian diet rather than the benefits.' He continued:

It is only in recent years that the non-vegetarian world has begun to recognize that in the vegetarian way of life there is probably a great deal that is of benefit to health. One particular aspect of this new-found importance of vegetarianism has gained especial prominence in recent years and initially led me to this study — and that is the importance of dietary fibre in health and disease.[1]

Emotional and intellectual benefits are also supposedly attributable to a vegetarian diet, according to a report in the American *Bulletin of the Psychonomic Society* for July 1977:

Recent data support the notion that vegetarian diets do in fact produce differences from meat-eating regimes in university examination performance with vegetarians scoring higher than meatarians and in the general area of emotionality . . . vegetable breakfasts produce less frustration and generally lower levels of irascibility than do meat breakfasts.

But for whatever reasons you give up meat, your new way of life *must* be based on knowledge. You do yourself and vegetarianism a dangerous disservice if you remain ignorant of simple nutritional principles, and an uninformed vegetarian is often worse off nutritionally than a carnivore. The first question to be faced is that of protein sufficiency.

Protein
It is still widely believed that meat is a 'first-class' protein and that giving it up will therefore result in having to accept 'second-class' substitutes. While there is a vague theoretical basis for this distinction it is not one that has any real relevance to a well-regulated vegetarian diet and is not now used by most nutritionists.

The distinctive feature of proteins is that, as well as carbon, hydrogen and oxygen, they all contain nitrogen. Man, as well as all other animals and most plants, cannot use nitrogen directly: plants require it in the form of nitrates in the soil, whilst Man and animals need it in the form of proteins. The two main functions of proteins are to promote structural growth and to repair worn or damaged tissue, and to maintain supplies of enzymes, hormones and antibodies.

Proteins are made up of amino acids, of which there are two

sorts — 'essential' and 'non-essential'. Essential amino acids are those which cannot be synthesized by the body and which must, therefore, be present in food. These are: methionine, tryptophan, lysine, leucine, isoleucine, phenylalanine, threonine and valine. Growing children need two more: arginine and histidine.

Non-essential amino acids, on the other hand, are those which the body can manufacture for itself. However, non-essential amino acids, in spite of their name, are every bit as essential as the essential amino acids.

Any protein that contains sufficient quantities of all the eight essential amino acids can be said to be a complete, or 'first-class', protein. It is true that animal proteins — meat, milk and eggs — meet this requirement and that plant proteins are generally deficient in one or more of the essential amino acids. Egg protein, for example, is almost completely utilized by the body and in fact is often taken as a reference point — i.e., its Net Protein Utilization (N.P.U.) is said to be 100 per cent.

The point is, however, that the distinction between complete and incomplete (or first- and second-class) proteins should not be made on the basis of individual cases; that is to say, plant proteins in combination can easily supply all the essential amino acids and can therefore be regarded collectively as providing a complete protein source that is in every way comparable to meat: 'If one takes beans and wheat together at one meal the N.P.U. value of the protein is almost equal to that of beef, which is 80 per cent. By combining vegetable proteins in one meal the resulting biological value is equal to most meats and sometimes greater.'[2]

Combination, then, is the key to protein sufficiency in a vegetarian diet. For example, several vegetable sources of protein are deficient in methionine, whereas most cereals contain a sufficient amount of this amino acid but are deficient in lysine. Seed and leaf proteins should therefore be eaten together and any animal proteins that are taken, such as eggs, cheese or milk, should be mixed with vegetable proteins at the same meal.

To ensure complete and correct utilization of the amino acids it is essential to combine proteins with carbohydrates — taken separately, the utilization of the nitrogen in the amino acids is affected. So eat them together — e.g., bread and cheese, nut roast and potatoes, macaroni and cheese, Welsh Rarebit, etc.

Vitamin B12

This is one of the most recently discovered vitamins and it is the only one to contain a metal — cobalt. Though only minute quantities are needed by the body (less than a millionth of a gram per day), vitamin B12 is of crucial importance.

There is a widespread belief espoused by popular nutritionalists that unless we eat animal products or swallow laboratory fabricated supplements, our bodies are in danger of developing pernicious anaemia due to vitamin B12 deficiency.

This is a tremendous hoax which has been created by research founded by the wealthy interests of the meat packing houses and processing plants. It is just another lie designed to frighten people into buying animal products.[3]

This is strong stuff and typical of the kind of shrill militancy that often antagonizes those it is meant to convert. But what of the substance of this claim? Can we really live without either animal sources or supplements of B12?

The article goes on to point out that vitamin B12 is heat and water soluble and that it is therefore lost when foods are cooked: 'Therefore, the addition of cooked meat or pasteurized dairy products to our diet will in no way prevent B12 deficiency anaemia . . .' How, then, can vegetarians and vegans obtain B12?

B12 is unique amongst vitamins in being produced by the activity of micro-organisms. It is then transmitted via animals and animal products to humans. Though it was once thought that no plant source with any significant amount of B12 existed, research has now shown that certain fermented soya foods (e.g. Tempeh) and some sea vegetables (e.g. Kombu) are rich in B12. It is also thought that we can synthesize B12 by means of a bacteria in our intestinal tracts, though beneficial flora can be destroyed by putrefactive organisms originating from meat, cooked foods and chemical preservatives. It is further thought that eating raw foods, organically grown, in proper combinations and avoiding chemically preserved foods will allow the natural synthesis of vitamin B12.

This is still a controversial view and many vegetarians and vegans feel safer taking B12 supplements. For the lacto-ovo vegetarian, milk, cheese and free-range eggs should provide sufficient B12, though, again, synthetic supplements will do no harm.

Calcium, Riboflavin and Iron
These, too, are potential problems for strict vegetarians, since milk is an important source of calcium and riboflavin. Living without milk and other dairy products therefore calls for strict dietary

surveillance.

Calcium is needed for the formation of teeth and bones and for ensuring that the blood clots and muscles function correctly. Recommended intake is about 1 gram per day, or 1.5 grams for children and expectant mothers. The main sources of calcium are milk, cheese, eggs, wholemeal bread, potatoes, watercress and cabbage.

Riboflavin is to be found in most green-leafed vegetables and in some cereals. It is soluble in water but it is not easily destroyed by cooking.

Iron is essential to the formation of haemoglobin, which carries oxygen to the tissues. Iron deficiency is not confined to strict vegetarians: many meat eaters suffer from it. In fact most vegetarians are better off in this respect because of their higher intake of foods that are rich in iron: unpeeled potatoes, raw vegetables, nuts, legumes and wholemeal bread.

Carbohydrates
These are in abundance in most moderate vegetarian diets. The principal sources are most vegetables, grains, fruits and sugars. The social and cultural correlations to carbohydrate sources are interesting: in the poorer countries of the world predominant carbohydrates differ significantly from those in more affluent countries. In Asia, for example, the predominant source is rice; in the U.S.A. processed sources, often sugar-based, predominate:

> In the United States the amount of carbohydrates in the daily diet has decreased by comparison with sixty years ago. More interesting yet is the type of carbohydrates that is being less often consumed. The amount of cereals, breads and potatoes in the diet has substantially decreased, while the use of sugars and sweets has gradually increased. This change in eating habits reflects not only the effects of technology, economy and the marketing system but also the inadequate nutritional status of many individuals.[4]

There is thus a crucial difference between valuable carbohydrates and those that are 'empty' (apart from their calories) and which contribute nothing of nutritional benefit to the diet.

The Anthropological Squabble
I have often found myself berated by a carnivore who insists that human beings were always omnivorous and that eating meat is

natural to his physical system. For him, vegetarians are straying from the norm, not carnivores.

But what is the truth? It is, of course, of fundamental importance to know what we were meant by nature to eat: if we can establish that, then we have a standard by which to measure and record any deviations. But is must be said that this is no easy task, though certain important clues are clear.

Our nearest relatives in the animal kingdom, chimpanzees and gorillas, are nearly all vegetarians — gorillas are completely so; chimpanzees, as Jane Goodall's observations on the Gombe Stream Reserve in what was Tanganyika in the 1960s showed, are occasional meat eaters, making about a dozen kills a year.

As far as hominids and prehominids are concerned, the evidence is still inconclusive, but observations of primitive hunting and gathering societies still in existence suggest that our ancient ancestors lived on a mostly vegetarian diet. Early hominids probably began to eat some meat in the form of abandoned carcases killed by animal predators or that had died naturally, but in the main, vegetable foods seemed to have formed the greater part of their diet.

With intellectual development, of course, the hunting of larger animals (a stage preceded by a certain amount of cannibalism) became common and Man developed into what he is now, an omnivore.

Physiologically, though, our vegetarian ancestry seems apparent. Our anatomy and bodily functions would seem to ally us, not with true carnivores, but with the frugivorous apes. In other words, meat eating is essentially an aberration to which our systems have accommodated themselves.

The following table outlines the main physiological differences between carnivores and vegetarians in Nature:

Carnivores	Vegetarians
1. Short bowels — for rapid expulsion of putrefactive bacteria.	1. Long bowels — for dealing with fermentative bacteria in vegetarian foods.
2. Long teeth and/or retractable claws for killing and holding prey.	2. Short teeth, no claws.
3. Jaws only open in an up and down motion.	3. Jaws move sideways for chewing.
4. Do not sweat through the skin. Body heat controlled by rapid breathing and extrusion of the tongue.	4. Sweat pores for heat control and elimination of impurities.
5. Saliva does not contain ptyalin and cannot pre-digest starches.	5. Saliva contains ptyalin for pre-digestion of starches.
6. Secrete large quantities of hydrochloric acid to dissolve bones.	6. Secrete little hydrochloric acid.
7. Lap water like a cat.	7. Take liquids in by suction through the teeth.

Three Vulgar Errors
The first of the three main errors about vegetarianism, that meat is essential for a 'proper' diet, has already been dealt with. The second error is that vegetarianism is an expensive alternative to eating meat. This is demonstrably not the case, and with more and more people growing their own vegetables it is certainly cheaper, even in an inflationary world, to live on a vegetarian diet than on a meat-based one. Vegetarianism, like anything else, has its luxuries and the health food trade has many tempting products to entice the weak of will. But if you can resist their blandishments your vegetarian diet should profit your purse as well as your health.

The third vulgar error is that vegetarian cooking is boring and uninteresting. A visit to the food and cookery section of any large bookshop will quickly dispel this myth. The dazzling variety of non-meat recipes will be instantly apparent. In the past vegetarianism may have been associated with an ascetic lifestyle and personal deprivation — but no longer:

> Intelligent vegetarianism today denies this traditional concept. It effectively negates the assertion that, since meat has long been the food of the prosperous, meat is therefore of all foods the most desirable . . . There is an infinity of difference between the serf's coarse black bread and limited supply of 'herbs' and the sophisticated array of artistically combined colours, delicate flavours, and varied textures of a modern vegetarian buffet.[5]

The best way, however, to convince people of the falsity of this error is the most obvious: cook for them. Once the palate approves, the rest is easy.

Priorities
Like people who go out of their way to rescue ill-treated donkeys, or who save kittens from drowning, or go to what some might see as extraordinary lengths to save the life of any animal, the vegetarian runs a high risk of being accused that his or her priorities are all wrong. Animals, the argument runs, are being held in more esteem than human beings and it is heard at its most vociferous and insistent in the vivisection debate.

Vegetarianism and vivisection are intimately related issues and the vegetarian must be prepared to be confronted on the question of experiments on live animals. 'To hold vivisection never justified', as Brigid Brophy has said, 'is a hard belief.'

> But so is its opposite. I believe it is never justified because I can see nothing (except our being able to get away with it) which lets us pick on animals that would not equally let us pick on idiot humans (who would be more useful) or, for the matter of that, on a few humans of any sort whom we might sacrifice for the good of the many.[6]

In any case, it is perfectly possible, or should be, to care for both human beings and animals: it is not really a case of mutually exclusive options, for on a global scale the adoption of a largely vegetarian diet would have considerable benefits for the majority of the human race. Growing crops to feed to animals, who are then slaughtered to provide human beings with protein, is a hopelessly inefficient system. On average, about 90 per cent of the protein in the plant foods that are fed to animals is used by the creatures themselves, leaving only about 10 per cent of the original protein value for those who eat their flesh. Ending this stupendous wastage and turning over land now used to grow animal feed to the cultivation of crops for direct human consumption would add immeasurably to the sum of human happiness.

But even if this were not true, the irresistible answer to the charge that vegetarians and anti-vivisectionists are somehow anthropomorphizing animals and lavishing their funds of human sympathy on inferior species lies precisely in the fact that animals *are* inferior to man's will and intelligence: 'The whole case for behaving decently to animals rests on the fact that we are the superior species. We are the species uniquely capable of imagination, rationality and moral choice — and that is precisely why we are under the obligation to recognize and respect the rights of animals.'[7]

The Subversive Process
Once you are familiar with all the obvious arguments and objections against your vegetarian way of life you should have the necessary confidence to move into the attack from time to time. Meal times present good opportunities, though tact and discretion are needed. Don't harangue your carnivores with every single mouthful. Wait until the meal is nearly over. If, as they should be, the occasional non-meat meals have been a success, the time is then ripe to exploit the feeling of well-being and contentment that always follows a good meal — meat or non-meat.

Few converts are made by verbal duels across the dinner table, but there may be quite a few made when the plates are cleared away and coffee, which vegetarians and carnivores alike can enjoy, is served. Good company in conjunction with delicious fleshless food can usually combine to convince where propaganda and preaching fail, and without resorting to fist-shaking, placards or soap boxes, much can be done in the way of subtle persuasion through food and good fellowship and, often the forgotten factor in the vegetarian controversy, a sense of humour.

So take advantage of the post prandial atmosphere and avoid being too assertive. Ask casually how your guests or your family enjoyed the meal. Some, of course, will say that it was all right but give them a nice juicy steak any time. Hard cases need a more

concerted treatment and it is often a good idea to work on them
first. If they are obviously satisfied and have admitted to enjoying
the non-meat meal, build on this: point out, gently, the variety of
vegetarian cookery; suggest that they might easily have half a dozen
vegetarian meals a week and still enjoy a Sunday roast.

Do not be over-zealous and be satisfied with small gains.
Realistically, you should not expect armies of converts after one
vegetarian meal. Your aim should be more modest: if you can
persuade your family and friends to cut down on their meat
consumption and eat a few vegetarian meals a week, you will have
done much.

Avoid emotional arguments — especially on the question of
animal rights. Avoid, too, downright abuse of the meat-eating
habit: it is not, after all, the darkest of sins but an aberration that
would be better corrected.

Be sure of your case. You may be emotionally and ethically
convinced of your cause but you need solid evidence as well. Hard
facts are your greatest allies: use them wisely.* Determined
carnivores are more likely to respond to one good, solid piece of
evidence, casually, dropped, than to a barrage of well meant but
ultimately ineffectual rhetoric. Statistics, for instance, are a good
gambit — e.g., 12,000 pigs a year die in transit to British slaughter-
houses, a loss in plain economic terms of between £600,000 and
£1.2 million a year.

Personal experience

Every now and again Fate lends you a helping hand and pulls off a
distinct and unexpected coup. The following is based on an actual
experience.

It was brought to the attention of a non-vegetarian friend over
dinner that contaminated meat is thought to be the main source of
salmonella poisoning in Britain and that conditions in slaughter-
houses encourage the proliferation of the salmonella pathogen. It
was mentioned almost casually and the conversation then veered off
on another topic. But some weeks later, after a take-away meal,
the friend in question found himself the victim of food poisoning
that was later diagnosed as salmonella. He makes the obvious
connection and the casual remark made over dinner became
suddenly significant.

* See Chapter 3.

Sudden Realization

A startling visual image — of calves muzzled from birth to prevent them from eating straw, which discolours their meat and makes it unmarketable — can also be a powerful catalyst. Shock tactics like this can be used occasionally to put euphemistic terms like veal, pork and beef firmly into perspective. Most non-vegetarians do not think of their favourite joints of meat as portions of decomposing flesh but as a kind of synthetic creation. Very often the establishment of a link between what goes into the mouth and where it actually came from in the first place can produce unexpected results. Many people just do not make the connection; if they did, if the reality of the creature that now lies dead on the plate before them and the conditions in which is passed its last hours were placed firmly before them, then little more argument would be necessary. Most people, when the facts become known to them, have been shocked into giving up meat. They just did not realize.

There is a deep fund of natural sympathy to be tapped by the vegetarian eager for converts. It would be to take an impossibly hard line to insist that everyone should be made to pay a visit to a slaughterhouse at least once in their lives, but somehow people need to be made aware of the processes that provide them with their Sunday joint. To bring this about, the subversive vegetarian needs to have access to a core of unsavoury but incontestable facts.

1. A report of Dr Gear's speech can be found in *Alive*, January/February 1979.
2. Dr Frey Ellis, late Consultant Haemotologist, Kingston Hospital.
3. Monica L. Rice, *Vegetarian Times*, September/October 1977.
4. Gary Null, *Protein for Vegetarians*, Pyramid, 1975, p. 52.
5. Shirley T. Moore and Mary P. Byers, *A Vegetarian Diet*, Woodbridge 1978, p. 22.
6. Brigid Brophy, *The Sunday Times*, 10 October 1965. Reprinted as 'The Rights of Animals' by The Vegetarian Society.
7. Brigid Brophy, *op. cit.*

3. FUEL FOR THE FIRE

At the outset, the subversive vegetarian faces a basic moral question: How far can one legitimately go in persuading other people to give up meat? This question cannot be dodged, though there is another, more teasingly philosophical, one: Is the turning away from meat a genetic compulsion, or the result of a rational decision?

Though the second question is more fundamental, the first has more immediate significance. The radical view is to assert that food habits can no longer be left to the whims of market forces and free enterprise; that dietary good sense must, in some way or other, be made to prevail; that, in a word, the right to eat badly is not inalienable. To the militant vegetarian, therefore, the right to eat what one pleases, if what pleases is the flesh of our fellow creatures, is not an absolute right.

A more moderate approach is to assume that it is people's ignorance that enforces the meat habit and that it is this that is the main stumbling block to a wider extension of the vegetarian way of life. If people knew more about the realities and the long-term viability of modern meat production, the argument might run, then they would make the 'right' choices of their own volition.

This is the essence of the subversive way: to place the right sort of information in the right way at the right time before people and try to make them look at their traditional assumptions about what they eat in a new way. Everyone rightly suspects the blood and thunder preacher with his purple prose and wagging finger. Vehemence is not the way. Gentler, more insidious means are needed. Persuading the world to give up meat, though, brings its own moral problems. Is it ethical to force people into doing something that they don't really want to do?

It is, after all, a conflict of freedoms: the freedom of certain types of animals to live out their allotted span without being slaughtered for food by human beings, and the freedom of the human animal to eat what pleases him. Some would say that there is no question at all; that the moral right of any creature to life is greater by far than the right of another creature to condemn it to live only for slaughter simply to gratify a perverted palate.

But it is by no means a clear cut issue, and once the argument for vegetarianism gets itself involved with fine ethical and moral distinctions, the practical, and in many ways more compelling, reasons for abandoning meat are submerged beneath a sea of speculative niceties.

On the assumption, then, that it is not unethical to make the ignorant wise, the subversive vegetarian can, with due discretion, allow himself to lighten the darkness of his carnivorous friends, allowing, wherever possible, the facts to speak for themselves.

Devil's Advocate
If vegetarians are sometimes timid in furthering their own cause, often with good reason, the meat trade is very much on the ball when it comes to spotting the weaknesses in its elaborate defence system. An example could be seen in the May 1977 issue of the *Meat Trades Journal,* which pointed to the kind of association meat producers do *not* want their customers to make: 'To acquaint the customer', it says, 'with the knowledge that the lamb chops she has just purchased were part of the anatomy of one of those pretty little creatures we see gambolling in the fields at springtime is probably the surest way of turning her into a vegetarian.' The cynicism is staggering, but the logic is perfectly sound.

The meat trade relies on this disassociation. It needs to keep the image of the animal in the field well away from the product it eventually becomes: the sausages and chops and rump steaks must in no way become associated with real pigs and sheep and cows.

It is hard to keep cool when one hears of people who take pleasure and make money through organized dog fights and people are justly horrified at the sight of a hare being ripped to pieces by greyhounds, or she-foxes savaged on a Saturday afternoon. Why, then, do those who feel disgust at these activities keep quiet at the horrors that are being perpetrated every day in their local slaughterhouse? Nor is there any essential difference to be made between the export of live calves to Europe and organized dog fights — except that we don't eat dogs. At least, not yet.

This confusion of values, made worse by the psychological

mechanism that disassociates meat products from real flesh and blood animals, is hard to overcome; but occasionally the anomalies it creates are highlighted dramatically.

New Forest Ponies

Take the case of the New Forest ponies. The outcry in 1978 over the slaughter of just one of them was considerable. 'Shoot Me, Not Pony, Pleads Hospital Girl' was one emotive headline. Gipsy, the horse that fourteen-year-old Kim Bowen kidnapped in a futile bid to save her from slaughter, tugged at a good many heart strings. In the wake of that story came the revelation that the best ponies and foals from the New Forest were being sold to be slaughtered — and then eaten by humans. Foal meat, said one enterprising gentleman, tastes very much like veal.

People were rightly disturbed and upset that the ponies were ending up on people's plates. In other words, they realized, or rather remembered, that living, breathing animals and 'meat' were not separate and distinct entities.

This is exactly what people generally do *not* do in the case of cows, sheep and pigs. Forcing people to make the identification should be a prime part of the subversive process. Why be shocked at the slaughter of pretty New Forest ponies when calves and lambs undergo a similar fate every single day? The rights of animals, like those of human beings, should be indivisible.

Keep a File

Almost every day a vigilant vegetarian, intent on building up a store of factual information, can find small snippets of great value in newspapers or magazines that can be filed away against the time when they can be marshalled against a particularly stubborn carnivore or perhaps used in defence of the vegetarian way of life.

Conviction must be backed up by hard facts. It is no good falling back on your feelings: people may occasionally admire the strength of your conviction, but the depth of your emotions will not usually bring them over to your side in eager droves. If you are cornered by a confident carnivore at a party you need to defend yourself with more than vague emotive appeals: with facts at your fingertips, however, you can turn a defensive position into an attack.

So keep a file. It need not be an elaborate system, just a folder containing press cuttings on relevant topics with the date and source noted on each. You need not confine yourself to just vegetarianism, for giving up meat usually involves a greater awareness of the need for dietary reform on a wide front. So look out for information on additives, potential carcinogens in food, chemical pollution affecting crops, and so on.

At home, if you are the only vegetarian in the family, the judicious use of hard facts can be extremely useful in lighting up those grey areas of habit and social conditioning on which many people base their opinions about food. Keep your eyes and ears open. There is so much that can be pressed into service.

Farming Methods

It is hard not to become emotional on the subject of modern intensive farming methods, but every vegetarian should try to keep a level head when discussing the subject: the calmer you can stay and the more your argument is backed up by hard facts, the more effective your case will be. Not that one can entirely deny one's feelings. No one, at least no one with a spark of decent feeling, can view the appalling conditions many factory-farm animals are subjected to with total objectivity. But it is far better to try and keep the emotional temperature low.

What follows has been based on my own file of cuttings gleaned from easily accessible sources over a year. Some of it makes unpleasant reading, but these things must be faced — as much by vegetarians as by meat eaters. If the carnivores amongst your family and friends are not aware of what is going on in these areas, then let them know — not aggressively, but, if possible, with tact and a sense of timing.

Choose the occasion well. Show them the actual cutting and let them read it for themselves. Ask them what they think about it. Above all, listen to them. Take an interest (at least feign an interest) in their point of view. Reveal the facts to them, but hold back from pontification: open their eyes and hope that natural human sympathy will do the rest.

Eggs for Breakfast

Eggs have a homely, comfortable image. They are redolent of warm childhood teas and breakfasts, with bread soldiers to kit out with helmets of yellow yoke. And of course they are an indispensable part of the traditional British breakfast.

But the realities of modern egg production and what happens to hens that have outlived their usefulness are far from homely. In November 1978 the *Sunday Telegraph* carried a report that nearly two million day-old chicks stood the risk of being gassed. The scheme had been put forward by United Kingdom Egg Producers, a Bristol-based organization, to try and increase the price of eggs by reducing the number of laying hens. The egg farmers represented by United Kingdom Egg Producers claimed that they were losing about 10p on every dozen eggs because shop prices were too low and production costs too high.

To the outsider, this seems an absurd situation. When years have been spent perfecting methods that can turn hens into efficient egg-laying machines (ignoring, for the moment, the awful means by which this efficiency is achieved), it seems ill-judged (to say the least) to complain that the system has worked too well by producing a surfeit of eggs and too many potential laying hens.

On top of all this was the desire to compound the cruelty of the battery system with the indiscriminate gassing of two million chicks — a process, like the extermination of baby seals, that was dignified with the euphemism 'culling'.

Mr John Pulman, Secretary of the United Kingdom Egg Producers, put the farmers' solution to the problem coldly and concisely: 'We feel the problem of over-production should be tackled at the source by restricting the number of laying birds. Gassing the chicks would be a simpler and cheaper method to do this'.[1]

The battery system is the main reason why most ovo-vegetarians try to eat only free-range eggs. The main official voice against the system is the Farm Animals Welfare Co-ordinating Executive (FAWCE), which represents organizations such as Compassion in World Farming, the Farm and Food Society, the Free Range Egg Group (FREGG), the R.S.P.C.A., Chickens' Lib, and the World Federation for the Protection of Animals.*

GECCAP (The General Election Co-ordinating Committee for Animal Protection), in their pamphlet *Putting Animals into Politics*, have come out strongly against the deep litter system, in which the space provided per hen is less than 1 square metre for laying hens and ½ square metre for broilers. On intensive animal husbandry in general it has this to say: 'In some respects existing standards recommended by the several Advisory Bodies concerned are below those in the Brambell Report more than ten years ago.'

* For further information about these and other organizations write to The Secretary, GECCAP, 10 Queensferry Street, Edinburgh EH2 4PG.

After the Eggs Have Stopped

In 1978 Lionel Hamilton-Renwick, an artist, was following a lorry on which were stacked crates containing live poultry. He was so distressed at the condition of the birds that, when the lorry pulled into a lay-by, he stopped to make a closer examination. What he saw made him instantly alert the local R.S.P.C.A. official and the police. 'I found that there were eighteen birds per crate,' he said. 'In one crate alone, three were dead. Altogether I counted ten dead, but as there were 4300 birds on this lorry piled six crates high, it was impossible to tell how many birds had been killed.'

The chickens were on their way to be slaughtered at a Suffolk poultry 'processing plant'. They were battery hens that had outlived their usefulness. It appeared that it is not illegal for such birds to be transported in this way for days on end, without food or water. These particular birds, according to Mr Hamilton-Renwick's description, were 'naked, most anaemic, and half dead'. He even had the strength of purpose to go to the processing plant where the chickens were unloaded and eventually slaughtered. It was, he said, 'the most horrifying sight I have ever witnessed.'[2]

The day after this appeared in the *Daily Telegraph* the same paper reported that two students, infiltrated into a poultry factory in Lincoln by the National Society Against Factory Farming, had amassed enough evidence for the Society to bring forty-five charges of cruelty against the factory. Among allegations of 'blatant torture' were the stubbing out of a cigarette in a chicken's eye, attempted strangulation, and the slitting of chickens' throats before they were stunned.

An eyewitness of the 'killing line' admitted disgust at what he saw: he said that many of the birds had deformed or swollen legs, many of which broke while they were being put into shackles prior to stunning.

'Glad I'm not a Pig', says Prince

Such were the reported words of the Prince of Wales after inspecting an experimental pig breeding unit at the National Agricultural Centre at Stoneleigh, Warwickshire, in 1978. In his capacity as President of the Royal Agricultural Society the Prince was shown pigs penned up with hardly enough room to move, and according to one report he made it clear to his guide that he did not approve of the system.

Little wonder. The Farm Animals Welfare Co-ordinating Executive has listed the following practices that they find unacceptable:

1. The close tethering of pigs except for a temporary purpose only (such as veterinary examinations).
2. The use of cubicles for dry or pregnant sows in which they are kept permanently and are unable to turn round.
3. Systems of pig husbandry where no form of bedding is provided and lighting is inadequate.
4. The castration of piglets destined for fattening for pork.[3]

The fact is, of course, that those involved in intensive animal husbandry only see animals in strict economic terms. They have to. The lives and deaths of farm animals are, after all, the basis of individual prosperity and the last thing people want to do is jeopardize their vested interests or their livelihoods. They cannot afford (literally) to be sentimental.

But there is a world of difference between what the factory farmer would perhaps call sentimentality and a humane attitude to downright cruelty. In other words, there is a balance to be struck between what can be legitimately used as the basis for a profitable living and what can be justifiably inflicted on a fellow creature. That balance has yet to be struck.

The complete divorce of animals as economic items from animals as sentient creatures is clearly shown by the following extract:

The pig, the common farm animal, has qualities which must be worthy of a place in the *Guinness Book of Records*. In just six months a pig can grow to 90 times its birthweight. A sow produces something like 1.8 tonnes of pig meat in 16 months (that's from conception to slaughter). And when it comes to slaughter there is so little waste. *As they say in the trade . . . the only part of a pig which can't be used is its squeak.*[4]

The article from which this extract is taken is a masterpiece of special pleading. 'Like all British meat', the writer glibly states, 'pork and bacon have most of the nutrients we need to stay healthy.' He continues:

They have protein and many minerals. The industry has invested much knowledge, a lot of cash and ambition, and, with so many EEC pressures, a lot of hope in its future ability to supply the British market. There's no question of its tremendous value. Like other British meat, it's got the lot.

It would be unkind, and irrelevant, to pick the writer up on his wayward syntax and grammar; but there are some things, to take up his claim of what pork and bacon have to offer, that pigs would be better off without.

Unsavoury Bacon

Pigs are particularly sensitive and vulnerable to stress. They can literally die of fright. Their flesh, when they are terrified in the slaughterhouse, becomes pale, soft and what is termed 'exudative'. Even before they reach the killing line the risk of death is high.

On the continent the situation is even worse. There pigs are often tranquillized to prevent transit-deaths. The drug used is called azaperone. Though the use of tranquillizers is illegal in Britain, because of possible carcase residues, the same drug, marketed under the name of *Stresnil,* is generally available.

Reviewing the overall drug situation in intensive farming in the *Veterinary Record,* Dr A. H. Linton, of the Bristol University Medical School, saw 'little indication that the overall scale of anti-biotics for veterinary use has decreased . . . As a consequence of intensive methods of husbandry, the prophylactic use of antibiotics to counteract some of the disease-risks involved is considered vital.'[5]

So what are the consequences of the widespread use of drugs in intensive farming? Quite simply, the danger that drug residues in carcases may have harmful effects on those who consume dead animals. Certain types of bacteria have become or are becoming drug-resistant, and this is not helped by conditions in slaughter-houses. According to Dr Linton, at least 52 per cent of bovine carcases and 83 per cent of pig carcases from commercial slaughter-houses are contaminated in one way or other. The intensive production of 'cheap' meat has therefore generated new strains of bacteria that can go on to play havoc in humans who eat contam-inated meat.

The Worm in the Bud

Meat eaters are often shocked to discover that their coveted Sunday joint might be a health hazard. It defeats all their assumptions and expectations; indeed the thought that meat could ever be anything other than a nourishing health-giving item of food has probably never crossed their mind.

But the consumption of animal fats is now being seen as a prime factor in the growing incidence of heart disorders; flesh foods are nearly always responsible for food poisoning;* and, as previously mentioned, intensive farming methods and the various drugs that now find their way into animals and animal foodstuffs may have incalculable long-term effects on human beings.

On top of all this there is evidence that infection by beef tapeworms, some of which may be up to ten feet long, is increasing in Britain. Tapeworm infection was practically unknown before the Second World War and even now it arouses little publicity because the worms actually do little physical damage to their human hosts, despite their horrific size.

In 1978 two scientists, Dr William Crewe and Dr Roderick Owen, both of the Liverpool School of Tropical Medicine, published an article on beef tapeworms in *New Scientist*. Though the symptoms of beef tapeworm infection in humans are comparatively trifling, even with worms that exceed forty feet, the situation is obviously not a satisfactory one. 'The implications are', said the article, 'that a considerable reservoir of tapeworm infection has already established itself in Britain.' It went on: 'Eradication would be difficult until the ways in which worms spread became known.'

There are several theories of how the worms spread. One view is that a single dropping from a bird that has recently fed on a sewage works and ingested a tapeworm segment could contain tens of thousands of tapeworm eggs.[6]

Cows Without Fields

The lorry drivers' strike in the U.K. during the winter of 1978/9 highlighted the precarious position of animals reared by intensive methods and which were wholly dependent on foodstuffs provided by their human masters. The strike hit pigs and poultry the hardest, but recent reports have indicated that the logic of intensive farming is now being carried to an alarming extremity in the production of milk from cows that are kept indoors all the year round and which are never allowed to graze for themselves in open fields.

The new system, much of the research for which has been carried out at the National Agricultural Centre in Warwickshire, involves feeding the cows computer-controlled rations made from tapioca,

---

* In 1975 there were 11,000 *reported* cases of salmonella poisoning in Britain. In 1978 a report by the British Association for the Advancement of Science said: 'Undoubtedly the greatest dangers arise from conditions in slaughterhouses. Contaminated meat is perhaps the main course of the pathogen's spread.'

bananas and various other cheap sources of vegetable waste.

As yet, the cows are not totally restricted within closed sheds, like battery hens or veal calves, and the buildings in which they are kept are, apparently, open-sided and the cows have freedom of movement within them. But they never eat grass, and they never experience the freedom of the open field.

In some versions of the system cows are being conditioned to respond to a bell that rings when mechanized food dispensers are ready to present them with individual rations: 'Each cow has a miniature transmitter around its neck which sends out a signal to a central control unit which is programmed to the animal's individual needs.'[7]

Isn't Nature wonderful?

Facts and Figures

Reports like these, then, are the fuel for the fire — the weapons a sensible vegetarian needs to have constantly at his fingertips. They have all been garnered from obvious sources and not from obscure esoteric journals. Use them judiciously; try to judge the right psychological moment before committing yourself to using them; above all, let the facts speak for themselves: do not attempt to build a sermon round them.

The facts and figures are there to be gathered and ignorance, after all, is your greatest enemy. No one now, for instance, seriously argues that smoking does not damage your health: the facts have been brought to everyone's attention. Take heart, then, from the fact that Sir Richard Doll, the distinguished Oxford professor of medicine who helped establish the smoking-lung cancer link, is now researching into the possible connection between meat eating and cancer.[8]

More and more weight of authority is being added to the claims for the beneficial nature of the vegetarian way of life: 'Food imports are, in fact, unnecessary. Our farm land is productive enough to support 250 million people on a vegetarian diet.' This confident pronouncement is not from a committed vegetarian source but from an editorial in the *British Medical Journal*. 'Anthropologists are still arguing about the proportion of meat in a "natural" human diet,' the editorial continues, 'but few nutritionists now dispute that western man eats too much meat, too much animal fat and dairy produce, too much refined carbohydrate, and too little dietary fibre.'[9]

The most vulnerable vegetarian is one who cannot fight back in what is still a hostile world. With an arsenal of facts, figures and authorities you can stand up for yourself when necessary and, just as importantly, you can begin to open the eyes of your carnivorous family and friends and begin to gently disabuse them of their fantasies about meat being the natural food of a truly civilized society.

1. *Sunday Telegraph,* 12 November 1978.
2. *Daily Telegraph,* 23 May 1978.
3. *Putting Animals Into Politics.*
4. Brian Kelly of the Meat and Livestock Commission in *Home Economics,* June 1978. My italics.
5. Quoted by Dr Alan Long, *New Vegetarian,* October 1977.
6. *The Times,* 3 November 1978.
7. *The Sunday Telegraph,* 7 January 1979.
8. Report in the *London Evening News,* 5 July 1977.
9. *B.M.J.,* July 1977.

4. BORROWED GLORY

We all like to think of ourselves as unique specimens. Something, we think, distinguishes us from everyone else. Even though we recognize bits of ourselves in others, the aggregate of physical features and that composite thing we call personality seem to us to form an inalienable individuality.

But sometimes it is comforting or flattering to submerge this proud consciousness of being unique; to allow ourselves the indulgence, merited or otherwise, of subsuming our opinions, beliefs, and even dreams, in those of others — particularly in those of people who have attained especial eminence. It pleases us to know that someone famous, or even infamous, thought as we do on a particular subject, and when engaged in argument it affords a peculiar strength to us to be able to cite celebrated authorities whose splendid and forceful utterances we borrow and quote without compunction, inwardly persuading ourselves that their words are, in some strange way, our own.

Illustrious vegetarians can be used in this way and this chapter examines a few of them, whose words and example may perhaps help the subversive vegetarian.

The Shelleyan Image
The vegetarian is an obvious figure of fun. W. S. Gilbert, for instance, attributed vegetarian ideals to the Aesthete in *Patience,* and they were clearly intended to be laughed at as a pretentious folly:

> Then a sentimental passion of a vegetable fashion must excite your languid spleen,
> An attachment *à la* Plato for a bashful young potato, or a not-too-French French bean.

Though the Philistines may jostle, you will rank as an apostle in
the high aesthetic band,
If you walk down Piccadilly with a poppy or a lily in your
mediaeval hand.
And everyone will say,
As you walk your flowery way,
'If he's content with a vegetable love which would certainly not
suit *me*,
Why, what a most particularly pure young man this pure young
man must be!'

The poet Shelley has become associated with this image of the
typical vegetarian as an effete and effeminate young man, but this,
fortunately for vegetarian propaganda, is a Victorian misconception.
    The falsification began with Mary Shelley, the poet's wife and
author of *Frankenstein,* who was constrained by the Shelley family
to suppress those aspects of her husband's life and character that
would strike mid-Victorian England as being in any way indiscreet,
whilst in the second generation Shelley's daughter-in-law, Lady
Jane Shelley, made it her life's work to establish what has been
called 'an unimpeachable feminine and Victorian idealization of
the poet.'[1]

The Real Shelley
Modern biographical research has revealed an altogether more
robust Shelley: hard, courageous, politically committed, learned,
witty, and occasionally cruel. His vegetarianism was the result, not
of a vague fad, but of real and carefully thought-out determination.
    His early espousal of vegetarianism was confirmed and strength-
ened by his meeting J. F. Newton, vegetarian, naturist and
Zoroastrian. In the long philosophical notes to *Queen Mab* (1813)
Shelley set forth his feelings about eating animal flesh:

I hold that the depravity of the physical and moral nature of
man originated in his unnatural habits of life . . . The allegory
of Adam and Eve eating of the tree of evil, and entailing upon
their posterity the wrath of God and the loss of everlasting life,
entails of no other explanation than the disease and crime that
have flowed from unnatural diet.

By 'unnatural diet' Shelley meant a meat diet. Following J. F.
Newton, he even explained the myth of Prometheus, the unfortunate
youth who stole fire from heaven and was chained for this crime to

Mount Caucasus, where a vulture continually devoured his liver, in terms of a change to a carnivorous diet:

How plain a language is spoken by all this! Prometheus (who represents the human race) effected some great change in the condition of his nature, and applied fire to culinary purposes; thus inventing an expedient for screening from his disgust the horrors of the shambles. From this moment his vitals were devoured by the vulture of disease. It consumed his being in every shape of its loathsome and infinite variety, inducing the soul-quelling sinkings of premature and violent death. All vice rose from the ruin of healthful innocence. Tyranny, superstition, commerce, and inequality were then first known, when reason vainly attempted to guide the wanderings of exacerbated passion.

This shows the passion of a young idealist, certainly; but Shelley's reasoning is not entirely without foundation. It is now widely accepted that there is a fundamental link between eating meat and certain kinds of disease, and it is salutary to recognize Shelley's argument in the following extract from a pamphlet issued by the Vegetarian Society: 'Cancer, tuberculosis and degenerative diseases of the heart are most prevalent in flesh-eating communities — the vegetarian Hunzas had no diseases of "civilization" until recently, when processed goods were introduced by kind-hearted Americans.' The pamphlet goes on: 'We think that Man may have degenerated into flesh-eating during the Ice Age when most of the vegetation was destroyed — butcher's shops and Eskimos living entirely on flesh are unhappy remnants of those catastrophic times.'

The Consequences of Cooking
Recent research in America has even hinted at a possible confirmation of Shelley's claim that the introduction of cooking, allied to the eating of animal flesh, was also associated with the proliferation of disease. Dr Barry Commoner, director of the Centre for the Biology of Natural Systems at Washington University, Missouri, has postulated the existence of what he has called 'culinary carcinogens'. In other words, he believes that cooking certain foods in certain ways can cause cancer. We remember Shelley's words on the consequences of Prometheus applying fire for culinary purposes: 'From this moment his vitals were devoured by the vulture of disease.'

Dr Commoner has discovered that well-cooked hamburgers and beef extract (the base for stock cubes) contain an as yet unidentified mutagen — a substance that reacts with DNA and causes changes in the way a cell reproduces itself. Most, though not all, mutagens are also carcinogens, i.e., cancer-inducing substances.

Beef tissue, and the stock that derives from it, do not, according to Dr Commoner, contain mutagens in any significant quantity until they are boiled: the more boiling they undergo, the more the mutagen count increases:

> As it was the *cooking* of the beef rather than the beef itself which appeared to be the source of the mutagen, Commoner went on to investigate a few common domestic cooking procedures. Quarter pound portions of lean ground beef were cooked in a 'home hamburger cooking appliance' for 90 seconds (rare), three minutes (medium) and five and a half minutes (well done). The rare hamburger was subsequently revealed to have only one part in a hundred millions of mutagen, but the mutagen content of the well done hamburger was fourteen times greater. Enough, Commoner claims, to cause concern.[2]

Japanese cancer researchers have also reported on mutagens: they found that meat and fish that were smoked or cooked at temperatures over 300°C (572°F) contained many more mutagens than the same foods in an uncooked state. Of related interest is the fact that Icelanders, who eat large quantities of smoked fish and sea birds, have a high incidence of stomach cancer.

It should in fairness be pointed out that Dr Commoner is not condemning meat as such: he merely points out the dangers of certain culinary processes. But as these processes are largely confined to the preparation of flesh foods and fish it is clear that meat eaters are more at risk than vegetarians. In this at least, Shelley's version of the Prometheus myth has an alarming relevance to the dietary habits of the twentieth century.

An Attachment à la Plato

The earliest indication of vegetarianism as an integral part of a wider philosophical view is to be found in ancient Greece. The first great figure known to have embraced a meatless diet was Pythagoras, who was, according to the Roman poet Ovid, 'the first to ban the serving of animal foods at our tables, first to express himself in such words as these . . . "O my fellow-men, do not defile your bodies with sinful foods . . . The earth affords a lavish supply of riches, of innocent foods, and offers you banquets that involve no bloodshed or slaughter." '[3]

The Roman historian Plutarch also referred back to the vegetarian beliefs of Pythagoras in graphic terms in his essay *On the
Eating of Flesh:*

> Can you really ask what reason Pythagoras had for abstaining
> from flesh? For my part I rather wonder both by what accident
> and in what state of soul or mind the first man did so, touched
> his mouth to gore and brought his lips to the flesh of a dead
> creature, he who set forth tables of dead, stale bodies and
> ventured to call food and nourishment the parts that had a little
> before bellowed and cried, moved and lived. How could his eyes
> endure the slaughter when throats were slit and hides flayed and
> limbs torn from limb? How could his nose endure the stench?
> How was it that the pollution did not turn away his taste, which
> made contact with the sores of others and sucked juices and
> serums from mortal wounds?[4]

The rhetoric is short on subtlety, but it certainly makes its point.

As for Plato, he and his master Socrates are usually considered to
have been vegetarians, though there is no direct evidence. The
simple life, however, was a central tenet of the Platonic ideal and
a 'natural' non-meat diet a significant part of that life.

Leonardo da Vinci

Leonardo has some claim to be the first modern vegetarian, though,
like everything else about him, the roots of his belief in a meatless
diet remain enigmatic and shrouded in mystery. 'He who does not
value life does not deserve it,' he said and, like Plutarch, he wrote
of the terrible barbarism that eating meat engenders: 'From count-
less numbers will be stolen their little children, and the throats of
these shall be cut, and they shall be quartered most barbarously.'

And yet this colossal, contradictory genius also designed an
ingenious piece of equipment for roasting meat, and this sensitive,
cultured humanist would coolly examine the fear-stricken faces of
condemned criminals in a spirit of absolute artistic detachment.

The vegetarian cause received notable theoretical support from
both the French essayist Montaigne and later by Jean Jacques
Rousseau, neither of whom, however, were practising vegetarians,
though both, like Sir Thomas More in *Utopia,* saw the ideal society
as existing on a meatless diet.

John Wesley and his brother Charles, as well as George White-
field and the prison reformer John Howard, were fervent and
influential eighteenth-century vegetarians. But it was not until the

closing years of the reign of Queen Victoria that vegetarianism acquired its most notable, and certainly most vocal, champion.

George Bernard Shaw

'It seems to me, looking at myself,' remarked Shaw in typical style, 'that I am a remarkably superior person, when you compare me with other writers, journalists, and dramatists; and I am perfectly content to put this down to my abstinence from meat. That is the simple and modest ground on which we should base our non-meat diet . . .'

George Bernard Shaw is easily the most celebrated, and the most vociferous, modern vegetarian. He took up vegetarianism in 1881 as a result of reading Shelley. Thereafter he spoke of meat-eating as 'cannibalism with its heroic dish omitted'.[5] He had three main objections to a carnivorous diet. First, he considered that animals were, in every sense, fellow creatures and that to slaughter and eat them was an abomination. He was careful, though, to distinguish between killing for food and killing for other reasons — self-defence, for example. His commitment was tempered by realism: 'We see the Buddhist having his path swept before him lest he should tread on an insect and kill it; but we do not see what the Buddhist does when he catches a flea that has kept him awake for an hour.'

Second, he saw flesh-eating as being socially harmful:

It involves a prodigious slavery of men to animals. Cows and sheep, with their *valetaille* of accoucheurs, graziers, shepherds, slaughtermen, butchers, milkmaids, and so forth, absorb a mass of human labour that should be devoted to the breeding and care of human beings. Some day, I hope, we shall live on air, and get rid of all the sanitary preoccupations which are so unpleasantly aggravated by meat-eating.

Third, Shaw related, like Shelley, the diminution of health and strength to eating meat. He referred to international athletes abstaining from eating scorched corpses and pointed to the bull, one of the strongest of animals and a vegetarian. Indeed he saw as one of the disadvantages of vegetarianism the accumulation of energy that was difficult to dissipate under normal conditions. 'What I want', he said, 'is a job of work. Thinning a jungle for preference. But whitewashing will serve.'

With his vegetarianism went abstention from alcohol and tobacco. Of the first he said, 'I am a teetotaller because my family has already paid the Shaw debt to the distilling industry so

munificently as to leave me no further obligations, and because my
mind requires no artificial stimulant . . . I flatly declare that a
man fed on whisky and dead bodies cannot do the finest work of
which he is capable.'

Shaw lived to be ninety-four on his vegetarian diet, though he
was careful to complement it with constant exercise. He also
managed to combine his dietary regime with a cuisine that was very
far from being primitive or 'back to Nature'.

> Some of the foods served at Ayot Saint Lawrence from 1943 on
> were: cheese strudel, soups such as vegetable, lentil, leek and
> tomato — all made without an animal-based stock — Russian
> salad, cucumber salad with yogurt, cream cheese and fruit salad;
> main dishes such as cabbage pie, zucchini au gratin, tomato and
> mushroom pie, stuffed aubergine, nut cutlets, lentil curry,
> poached eggs and rice, numerous sauces such as walnut, cran-
> berry, apple, bread, tartar and gooseberry; and desserts that
> included baked apples stuffed with almonds, vanilla, strawberry
> and coffee ice cream, lemon mousse, baked bananas, and apricot
> mould.[6]

Late in life Shaw took liver extract to counteract a haemoglobin
deficiency, which, when it became generally known, caused some
consternation and anger among hard line vegetarians. In a letter to
Symon Gould, founder of the American Vegetarian Party, which
was printed in the *American Vegetarian*, Shaw stoutly defended
his apparent lapse in a strongly practical manner:

> Liver extract you would take if you developed pernicious
> anaemia. If you were diabetic you would take insulin. If you had
> oedema you would take thyroid. You may think you wouldn't;
> but you would if your diet failed to cure you. You would try any
> of the gland extracts, the mineral drugs, the so-called vaccines, if
> it were that or your death.

Shaw's self-confidence is infectious and inspiriting. For any
vegetarian who is facing a crisis of confidence and who needs to be
confirmed in his beliefs (as we all do from time to time) there is no
finer tonic than Shaw's sublime egoism.

Dons, Dictators and Cranks

Vegetarianism has certainly attracted its fair share of eccentrics —
and undesirables. Affiliated to the great vegetarian eccentrics was
the Rev. C. L. Dodgson, of Christ Church, Oxford, otherwise

known to the world as Lewis Carroll. Though not a vegetarian, Dodgson did pronounce, amongst a myriad other topics, on vivisection. In his pamphlet *Some Popular Fallacies About Vivisection* he commented on the following proposition: 'That man is infinitely more important than the lower animals, so that the infliction of animal suffering, however, great, is justifiable if it prevent human suffering, however small'.

This fallacy can be assumed only when unexpressed. To put it into words is almost to refute it. Few, even in an age where selfishness has almost become a religion, dare openly avow a selfishness so hideous as this! While there are thousands, I believe, who would be ready to assure the vivisectors that, so far as their personal interests are concerned, they are ready to forego any prospect they may have of a diminution of pain, if it can only be secured by the infliction of so much pain on innocent creatures.[7]

As for the argument that human and animal suffering differ in kind, Dodgson deftly parried it with an appeal to the prevailing Darwinism. It is inconsistent, he says, to maintain, on the one hand, that 'man is twin-brother to the monkey' whilst holding, on the other, that both experience pain in a different way. 'Let them be at least consistent,' he concluded 'and when they have proved that the lessening of the *human* suffering is an end so great and glorious as to justify any means that will secure it, let them give the anthropomorphoid ape the benefit of the argument. Further than this I will not ask them to go, but will resign them in confidence to the guidance of an exorable logic.'

The most infamous undesirable in the vegetarian cause was, of course, Hitler. 'Did you know that Wagner had attributed much of the decay of our civilization to meat-eating?' Hitler asked Hermann Rauschning in 1933. Wagner did not, however, practise what he preached: for him, vegetarianism was for the perfect world, not for this one. But nonetheless, he was instrumental in making a practising vegetarian out of Adolf Hitler, who believed that what he saw was the 'decay' of modern civilization had its origins in the abdomen.

Hitler's vegetarianism is an unpleasant fact to be faced by the subversive vegetarian: it is an obvious but nonetheless effective rejoinder to conversion attempts for a carnivore to point to Hitler and say, 'If that's what vegetarianism does for you, the world's better off eating meat.' It might seem untenable for a vegetarian to argue that eating meat has an adverse effect on the moral nature and that it coarsens and blunts the sensibility when a man like Hitler spent most of his life avoiding flesh foods, and in a way it is. Faced with the example of Hitler one can only maintain that the rights and wrongs of killing animals for food have nothing to do with the accident of Hitler's vegetarianism. No one, after all, could seriously argue that Hitler was what he was *because* of his eating habits.

Finally, there are the cranks, the various sects and minority groups who have embraced vegetarianism as a radical alternative to the acquisitive materialist world around them. Sects such as the Doukhobors, who, fired with the high ideals of Tolstoy, migrated from Czarist Russia to the wide wheatlands of Canada to practise their ascetic brand of vegetarianism and organize nude protest marches. Latterly, there has been a vague association of vegetarianism with hippiedom, that joss-stick infested world of brown rice, beads and universal love. And though flower power may have died its spirit lives on in the gentle but inadequate philosophy of macrobiotics.

You Are Not Alone

Even this brief and incomplete sketch should have shown the value to the subversive vegetarian of knowing something about the tradition of which he is a part. In spite of all the cranks and the obvious eccentrics (types just as common, indeed more so, amongst carnivores), vegetarianism has attracted a large number of notable figures. It is as well to know just a little, at least, about them. For one thing, it will improve your powers of argument to have knowledge, however slight, of historical precedents.

But, more importantly, knowing that you are not alone, that you are part of a long and distinguished line, should help to boost your morale and give you all the confidence you need when faith, as it sometimes does, begins to falter.

1. Richard Holmes, *Shelley: The Pursuit* (1974), xi.
2. *Sunday Times*, 17 September 1978.
3. Ovid, *Metamorphoses*, translated by Mary Innes, Penguin 1973.
4. Plutarch, *Moralia*, translated by H. Cherniss and W. C. Helmbold, 1957.
5. The quotations in this section are from Hesketh Pearson, *G.B.S. A Full Length Portrait*, 1942.
6. Janet Barkas, *The Vegetable Passion*, RKP (1975), p. 94.
7. Lewis Carroll, *Some Popular Fallacies About Vivisection*, in *Lewis Carroll: The Complete Works*, Nonesuch Press (1977).

5. SUBVERSIVE RECIPES

The subversive process so far has been based on the acquisition of information. You need to be reliably informed, both to defend yourself from criticism and to convince where ignorance is perhaps your greatest enemy.

This chapter deals with the most obvious way to convince people that a reduction of their meat intake is not *ipso facto* a deprivation: cook for them.

A word is due on the inclusion of fish and dairy products in the recipes and on the nature of the recipes themselves. The basic aim is to *satisfy* habitual carnivores and to make them feel that in giving up meat (even if only for a few meals a week) they are not losing out on anything. Substantial, filling meals are therefore the prime objective.

The recipes that follow are in no sense *haute cuisine:* they are for basic, nourishing non-meat meals that can be prepared easily and that require no exotic ingredients or special skill. They are designed to blend in with a traditional meat-based diet, not stand in opposition to it. This way, carnivores feel less nervous about giving up meat: by becoming an accepted part of their dietary routine, non-meat meals seem less like radical innovations.

By including dairy products and fish, this can be accomplished more easily. It may not be what strict vegetarians would advocate, but then they have already committed themselves. These recipes are for people for whom the choice between eating meat and becoming a vegetarian is by no means an easy or obvious one and who feel apprehensive, frightened, or even hostile, at the thought of changing their traditional dietary pattern. The subversive vegetarian should make things as easy as he can for the carnivores he is working on — no matter what hard line vegetarians may think.

The Middle Way

It is a truism that there are as many vegetarian diets as there are reasons for giving up meat, hence those cumbersome categories that some people are so fond of using — lacto vegetarians, lacto-ovo vegetarians, ovo-vegetarians, vegans, and so on. Inevitably, when people divide themselves up this way, there is a tendency for one group to look down on or openly disapprove of another and perhaps to label those who do not toe their particular ideological line as 'pseudo-vegetarians'.

But this lack of charity is totally destructive. If people wish to eat meat, then they have a perfect right to do so — perhaps not an absolute moral right, but certainly a democratic one. If these people can be persuaded to give up at least some meat, even if it means that they replace it with fish and dairy products, the result must be worth striving for.

It will never be a totally vegetarian world; that, unfortunately, is a dream. But there is perhaps a real possibility that meat consumption could be reduced — to the lasting benefit of man and beast.

SOUPS

Soups can (indeed, often should be) meals in themselves, with fresh brown bread, cheese and perhaps a side salad to complete the nutritional balance. They can be prepared in advance and perhaps even taken to work in a flask in an attempt to counteract the pie and pint syndrome. They are also ideal for those who have to snatch a quick lunch at home, being filling and nourishing without blowing you out for the rest of the afternoon.

So try seducing your carnivores away from ham and chips with a few home-made non-meat soups. Ideas are plentiful: here are just a few.

Basic Stock
Green vegetable water, which can be saved and stored in the refrigerator, makes a perfectly good basic stock. If you need to make up some stock simply dissolve a teaspoonful of Marmite in about ¾ pt. (425ml) of warm water.

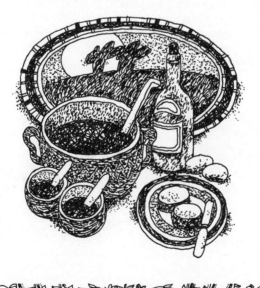

Basic Vegetable Soup

½ lb (225g) of fresh tomatoes
1 large onion
1 carrot
1 small swede
1 turnip
1 medium-sized potato
1 medium-sized parsnip
1 cupful of red kidney beans (cooked)
1 cupful of macaroni, spaghetti or noodles
1½ pt. (825ml) basic vegetable stock
1 teaspoonful of Marmite

Peel and prepare all the vegetables and chop into even-sized pieces. Melt some margarine in a saucepan and *sauté* the onion for a few minutes. Add the carrot, followed by the turnip and the swede, and continue to cook gently for 2-3 minutes. Finally, add the parsnip and the potato.

Cover with the stock and season. Add the chopped tomatoes, cover and cook slowly until all the vegetables are tender (about 30 minutes).

Add the pasta of your choice, the kidney beans and the Marmite and cook for a further 10-15 minutes.

Serve with grated cheese.

Easy Vegetable Soup

½ lb (225g) of potatoes
2 large carrots
1 medium-sized onion
3 sticks of celery
1½ pt. (825ml) of basic vegetable stock or water
A few outer cabbage leaves
1½ oz. (40g) margarine
½ teaspoonful of marjoram
2 teaspoonsful of Marmite or yeast extract

Wash the vegetables. Cut the cabbage leaves into narrow strips and peel and cube the carrots, potatoes, onion and celery sticks.

Melt the margarine in a heavy-based saucepan, *sauté* the carrots for a few minutes and then add the celery followed by the cabbage and the onion. Cover and cook gently for about 10 minutes, stirring occasionally.

Add the potatoes and cook for a further 5 minutes. Then add ½ pt. (275ml) of basic vegetable stock (or water) and cook until the vegetables are nearly tender.

Add the rest of the stock, together with the marjoram, Marmite or yeast extract and seasonings to taste. Cook for 5 minutes.

Serve sprinkled liberally with grated cheese.

Cream of Spinach Soup

½ lb (225g) of chopped spinach
1 large onion
2 oz. (50g) of margarine
2 oz. (50g) 81% stoneground flour
1 pt. (550ml) basic vegetable stock or water
1 pt. (550ml) of milk
Salt
Grated nutmeg

Cook the chopped spinach. Peel and cut the onion up finely and *sauté* in the margarine until it is golden-brown.

Add the flour and cook for 5 minutes, stirring all the time. Add the stock or water and the milk and cook for a further 10 minutes. Finally, add the spinach, salt and a pinch of grated nutmeg.

Lentil Soup

2 oz. (50g) of lentils
¾ pt. (425ml) of boiling water
1 carrot
1 large onion
1 clove of garlic
1 teaspoonful of cornflour
¼ pt. (150ml) of milk
Salt and pepper

Rinse the lentils in cold water and soak them in boiling water for an hour. Bring back to the boil and skim. Add the peeled and sliced onion, carrot and garlic clove.

Simmer for about an hour and then pass through a sieve or put into a blender. Thicken with the flour that has been blended with the milk.

Season, reheat and serve.

Potato and Leek Soup

1 large onion
2 medium-sized leeks
2 large potatoes
1 tablespoonful of margarine
1½ pt. (825ml) of vegetable stock or water
½ bunch of watercress
Top of the milk (if needed)
Salt and pepper

Slice the onion and the leeks and *sauté* in the margarine in a large saucepan, taking care they do not brown. Peel, dice and add the potatoes. Cover the saucepan and cook gently for about 5 minutes.

Add the vegetable stock or the water and the seasonings and simmer until the potatoes are tender. Liquidize or put through a sieve. If the soup is too thick, add top of the milk as necessary.

Serve with a swirl of single cream and garnish with freshly-chopped parsley or watercress.

This soup, like the two that follow, is delicious chilled and makes a welcome change in the summer from salads.

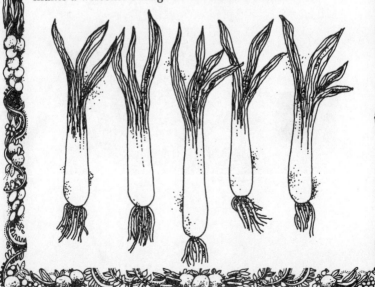

Chilled Carrot Soup

1¼ lb (550g) of young carrots
1 medium-sized onion
3 garlic cloves
1 oz. (25g) of margarine
2 pt. (1¼l) of vegetable stock or water
8 fl. oz. (225ml) of double cream
Salt and black pepper
Parsley to garnish

Peel and thinly slice the onion and the garlic cloves. Melt the margarine in a saucepan and add the onion and the garlic. Cook over a low heat, keeping the pan covered, until the onion is soft and transparent.

Meanwhile, scrape the carrots and chop them thinly. Add them to the onion and the garlic and cook for about 8 minutes. Add the stock and simmer for a further 30 minutes.

Allow to cool and liquidize, or sieve, until smooth. When it is cool, add the cream, the salt, and the black pepper. Chill for at least an hour before serving, garnished with chopped parsley and a swirl of cream.

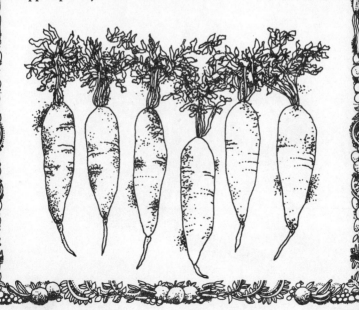

Watercress Soup

4 or 5 bunches of watercress
1 medium-sized onion
4 medium-sized potatoes
2 oz. (50g) of margarine
1 pt. (550ml) of milk
Salt and black pepper

Slice the onion and peel and quarter the potatoes. Melt 1 oz. (25g) of the margarine in a saucepan and add the onion and potatoes. Cover and cook gently over a low heat for about 10 minutes, making sure that the vegetables do not brown.

Clean and strip the leaves from 4 bunches of watercress and add to the onion and potatoes. Add the seasonings and enough water to cover. Cover the pan and cook until the potatoes are tender.

Add the milk and the remaining bunch of watercress and cook for a further 5 minutes. Liquidize or sieve the soup and reheat, adding the remaining margarine and a squeeze of lemon juice.

This, too, is delicious chilled.

French Onion Soup

¾ lb (325g) of onions
2 oz. (50g) of margarine
1 tablespoonful of 81% stoneground flour
2 pt. (1¼ l) warm water
1 teaspoonful of Marmite
Salt and freshly-ground black pepper
1 tablespoonful of red wine

Peel and slice the onions and drop them into a saucepan in which the margarine has been melted. Make sure that the pan is really hot and shake well so that the onions are nicely coated with the melted margarine. Adjust the heat so that they brown gently and be careful not to let them blacken.

Stir in the flour until this too is browned (about 4 minutes). Take off the heat and very gradually add the warm water into which the Marmite has been dissolved. This must be done carefully to avoid lumpiness.

Bring back to the boil, add the salt and black pepper and allow to simmer with the lid on for 20 minutes. Just before serving add the tablespoonful of red wine, but do not reheat after you have done this or the wine will turn bitter.

Serve with croutons of toasted cheese squares.

Chestnut Soup

½ lb (225g) of chestnuts
1 medium-sized onion
2 oz. (50g) of celery
1 small carrot
¼ teaspoonful of salt
¼ teaspoonful of brown sugar
1 oz. (25g) of margarine
½ pt. (275ml) of vegetable stock
½ pt. (275ml) of creamy milk
Sprig of thyme and parsley

Melt the margarine in a heavy pan. Shell the chestnuts and slice the vegetables thinly. Add them to the melted margarine and leave to brown slightly before adding the heated stock, the salt, sugar and the herbs.

Allow to simmer for an hour and then strain the liquid into a bowl and press the chestnuts and the vegetables through a sieve. Pour the liquid back over the chestnut and vegetable *purée,* stirring all the time. Simmer for 5 minutes.

Just before serving, add the creamy milk and top with parsley.

An evocative, warming, winter soup.

VEGETABLE DISHES

There are two golden rules to observe when cooking all vegetables: do not oversoak and do not overcook. In fact, as regards the first, it is best not to soak at all: steaming or (better still) *sautéeing* are much better.

In meat cookery, vegetables are relegated to side positions. Here are some recipes that make them the centre of attraction and give carnivores that feeling of being full and well-nourished that they so prize.

Vegetable Chop Suey

½ head of cabbage
2 large onions
2 large carrots
½ lb (225g) of fresh bean sprouts
2 or 3 sticks of celery
3 tablespoonsful of vegetable oil
4 tablespoonsful of water
½ teaspoonful of yeast extract or Marmite
2 tablespoonsful of soy sauce
2 teaspoonsful of cornflour
2½ cupsful of vegetable stock
1 teaspoonful of ground ginger
Salt

Peel and slice the carrots and the onions. Cut the celery and the cabbage into inch-long pieces. Heat the vegetable oil in a heavy-based saucepan (a Chinese wok is best), add the vegetables and stir well so that they are covered by the oil. Cover and cook gently for 3 minutes.

Add the stock and simmer for a further 3 minutes, then add the soy sauce and the yeast extract (or Marmite). Blend the cornflour and water and add to the vegetables. Cook gently for 5 minutes.

Finally, add the bean sprouts. Stir thoroughly and add some more stock (or water) if the mixture is too thick. Serve with brown rice.

Remember, it is absolutely essential not to overcook the vegetables.

Vegetable Curry

1 large onion
3 or 4 medium-sized potatoes
1 small cauliflower
2 medium carrots
1 generous tablespoonful of curry powder
3 tablespoonsful of vegetable cooking oil
2 oz. (50g) of 81% stoneground flour
¾ pt. (425ml) of stock made by seeping 4 oz. (100g)
of desiccated coconut in boiling water for 15 minutes
and then straining
2 tablespoonsful of lemon juice
Salt and pepper

Peel and chop the onion and break the cauliflower into florettes. Peel and dice the potatoes and slice the carrots. Heat a little of the oil in a large heavy-based saucepan, add the onion, and fry until well browned.

Add the flour and cook for a few moments and then add the curry powder. Put in the rest of the prepared vegetables and stir well, making sure that the mixture is well covered with curry and oil.

Cover the pan and *sauté* for 5 minutes and then pour the strained coconut stock over the mixture. Season to taste and allow to simmer gently until the vegetables are tender. Add the lemon juice just before serving.

Curries are best prepared early in the day, or even during the previous one, and left to allow the flavours to mingle and be thoroughly absorbed. However, reheat carefully to avoid breaking up the vegetables.

Fruity Curry

½ lb (225g) of brown rice
½ lb (225g) of split peas
2 medium-sized onions
2 large cooking apples
2 bananas
1 teaspoonful of lemon juice
1 tablespoonful of curry powder
1 tablespoonful of chutney
1 oz. (25g) of desiccated coconut
2 oz. (50g) of raisins or sultanas
1 garlic clove
Salt and pepper

Wash the split peas and soak them overnight in the refrigerator (this will shorten the cooking time). Cook the brown rice in a tightly-covered pan for 45 minutes and then keep warm.

Strain the split peas, put into a saucepan and cover with boiling water. Boil until soft (about ¾ hour). Add the chopped and peeled onions, apples and bananas, the curry powder, garlic and raisins (or sultanas). Simmer for a further ¼ hour and then strain.

Add the lemon juice and chutney and taste for seasonings. Turn onto a hot serving dish, sprinkle with coconut and surround with the cooked brown rice.

Vegetable Pie

½ pt. (275ml) of cheese sauce
2 small carrots
2 parsnips
½ medium-sized swede
1 small turnip
1 onion
2 medium-sized leeks
4 oz. (100g) of runner beans (or peas, if preferred)
1½ lb (675g) of medium to large potatoes

Peel and slice, or dice, all the vegetables (unless, of course, you are using peas) finely. Boil them in a small amount of salted water, adding the carrots a few minutes before the others as they take longer to cook.

Meanwhile, prepare and cook the potatoes separately. When they are almost tender, drain and slice them thinly. When the other vegetables are cooked, drain them and place in a large, shallow, ovenproof dish. Pour the cheese sauce over them and mix thoroughly.

Lay the sliced potatoes in neat rows over the vegetable and sauce mixture. Dot with margarine and sprinkle liberally with sea salt and black pepper.

Cook in a hot oven for 10-15 minutes and then, if the potatoes are not browned, place under a medium grill.

Garnish with chopped parsley.

Vegetable Charlotte

1 cupful of *puréed* carrots
1 cupful of *puréed* turnips (or parsnips or swedes)
1 cupful of *puréed* brussels sprouts
6 slices of brown bread
Margarine

400°F (204°C/Gas Mark 5)

Spread the slices of brown bread with the margarine and cut into fingers. Line a greased baking dish or pudding basin with the bread, reserving enough to cover the top.

Mix the *puréed* vegetables together and place in the dish. Cover with the remaining bread and bake for 30 minutes.

Savoury Lentil Roast

1 medium-sized onion
2 oz. (50g) of margarine
½ lb (225g) of lentils
1 bay leaf
3 oz. (75g) of cooked brown rice
1 clove of garlic
2 eggs (free-range)
6 oz. (175g) of grated cheddar cheese
4 oz. (100g) of brown breadcrumbs
1 teaspoonful of Marmite
Black pepper to taste

300°F (149°C/Gas Mark 3)

Wash and soak the lentils for ¾ hour in boiling water. Peel and chop the onion and *sauté* in the margarine. Put the strained lentils into a large saucepan with the bay leaf and ½ pt. (275ml) of cold water. Bring to the boil and simmer for ¾ hour.

Remove the bay leaf and stir in the Marmite. Beat the eggs, crush the garlic clove and combine all the ingredients. Pack the mixture into a greased loaf tin and cook for 30 minutes.

Serve hot with a thick gravy made with vegetable stock thickened with flour and browned and seasoned with Marmite.

Spiced Lentils

½ lb (225g) of lentils
2 oz. (50g) of margarine
1 large garlic clove
1 medium-sized onion
1 teaspoonful of ground coriander
½ teaspoonful of ground ginger
½ teaspoonful of ground cumin
¼ teaspoonful of ground chilli
¼ teaspoonful of ground turmeric
½ teaspoonful of sea salt

Peel and chop the onion and then *sauté* gently in the margarine. Crush the garlic and mix with the rest of the spices. Wash and drain the lentils and add to the *sautéed* onion. Cook gently for 5 minutes, stirring occasionally.

Pour 1½ pt. (825ml) of hot water over the mixture, cover, and allow to simmer for about ½ hour, or until the lentils are soft. Add more seasonings if necessary.

Tian of Onion

3 lb (1¼kg) of large sweet onions
5 tablespoonsful of olive oil
2 oz. (50g) of 81% stoneground flour
8 oz. (225g) of brown breadcrumbs
Nutmeg
Salt and pepper

300°F (149°C/Gas Mark 3)

Brown the breadcrumbs in 1 tablespoonful of olive oil. Peel and slice the onions and cook in boiling salted water until tender. Drain, but keep the liquid. Make a sauce using the olive oil blended with the flour. Gradually add a little milk and about 8 fl. oz. (225ml) of the onion liquid so that the sauce becomes the consistency of double cream. Season with salt, pepper and nutmeg.

Grease an ovenproof dish lightly with olive oil and pour in just under half of the sauce. Cover with the cooked onion slices. Pour the remaining sauce on top and sprinkle with the browned breadcrumbs.

Bake in the oven for about ½ hour until it is well browned.

Stuffed Onions

4 large Spanish onions
2 tablespoonsful of brown breadcrumbs
1½ oz. (40g) of margarine
2 oz. (50g) of grated cheddar cheese
1 tablespoonful of chopped mixed nuts
Made mustard to taste
Salt and pepper

325-350°F (163-177°C/Gas Mark 3)

Peel the onions but do not cut off the bases. Boil them gently for about 30 minutes until the outsides are tender. Lift them out of the water and allow to cool.

Carefully remove the centres, chop them finely, and add them to a mixture of the breadcrumbs, cheese, margarine, nuts and seasonings. Fill each cavity with the mixture and place on a well-greased baking tray and cook for about 1 hour or until browned.

Courgettes Riccioni

**1 large onion
1 lb (450g) of courgettes
1 oz. (25g) of margarine
3 eggs (free-range)
1 teaspoonful of top milk
Salt and pepper**

Wash the courgettes and slice them lengthways into thin strips. Then chop them finely. Peel and dice the onion and fry gently in the margarine with the courgettes until they become a light golden-brown.

Beat the eggs with the milk, add salt and pepper to taste and a pinch of mixed herbs. Pour over the browned onions and courgettes. Leave on a low heat until the eggs are set.

Brown the top under a hot grill and garnish with parsley.

Parsnip Pie

2 lb (900g) of parsnips
1 lb (450g) of tomatoes
3 oz. (75g) of margarine
3 oz. (75g) of soft brown sugar
6 oz. (175g) of grated cheese
¼ pt. (150ml) of single cream
1 cupful of fresh brown breadcrumbs

325°F (163°C/Gas Mark 3)

Peel the parsnips and remove any hard cores. Slice thinly and fry lightly in a little oil for about 4 minutes.

Slice the tomatoes. Grease an ovenproof dish and lay a layer of sliced parsnips in it and sprinkle with salt, pepper, a little brown sugar and cream. Then cover with a layer of sliced tomatoes. Sprinkle these with grated cheese and repeat these layers, finishing with the tomatoes and cheese.

Sprinkle breadcrumbs on the top and dot with margarine, pepper and salt. Cook for about 40 minutes in the centre of the oven.

Cauliflower Cheese

1 medium-sized cauliflower
½ pt. (275ml) of milk
2 oz. (50g) of margarine
2 oz. (50g) of 81% stoneground flour
1 teaspoonful of mixed mustard
4-6 oz. (100-175g) of grated cheese
Salt and pepper

Cook the cauliflower florettes in boiling salted water until they are tender. Meanwhile, make a cheese sauce by melting the margarine and flour, adding the milk gradually, and then bringing to the boil. Simmer for a few minutes, then add the cheese, reserving a little to add to the top of the cauliflower. Add the seasonings, stir well and cook until the cheese has melted.

Drain the cauliflower and place in an ovenproof dish. Pour the sauce over it and sprinkle the top with the remaining cheese.

This recipe can also be used for macaroni cheese simply by substituting 4 oz. (100g) of uncooked macaroni for the cauliflower.

Cauliflower cheese is a simple and economical dish which is nonetheless filling and nutritious and which can feed the troops quickly and efficiently.

Hot Button Mushrooms

1¼ lb (550g) of button mushrooms
1 medium-sized onion
A little oil
2 oz. (50g) of margarine
2 oz. (50g) of 81% stoneground flour
½ pt. (275ml) of single cream
2 eggs (beaten)
White wine
Salt and pepper

Clean and chop the mushrooms. Dice the onion and *sauté* with the mushrooms in the oil. Put a few mushrooms aside for garnishing.

Add the flour to the remaining mixture and cook, stirring all the time. Mix the cream, the beaten eggs, white wine and seasonings together and add to the mushroom mixture. Allow to cool. Then pour into a prepared pastry case and bake for about 30 minutes.

Garnish the top with the mushrooms you have saved and a few sprigs of parsley. Serve hot.

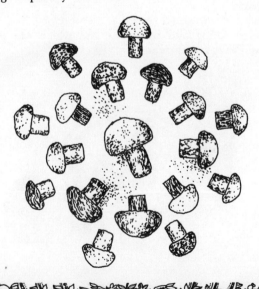

Cabbage Pie

1 medium-sized white cabbage
4 oz. (100g) of margarine
2 hard-boiled eggs
6 oz. (175g) of cheddar cheese
Milk
Pastry (short or flaky), enough to line and cover
a 9-inch pie dish
Salt and pepper

350-375°F (177-191°C/Gas Mark 4)

Shred the cabbage finely. Melt the margarine in a large saucepan and add the shredded cabbage to it. Cook gently for about 5 minutes.

Line the pie dish with pastry and then build up alternate layers of cabbage, slices of hard-boiled egg, and cheese, seasoning each layer as you go. Repeat until the dish is full with a pastry topping.

Brush the top with milk and bake for about 30 minutes.

Dolmades

2 oz. (50g) of long grain brown rice (uncooked)
1 lb (450g) of courgettes
1 tin of tomatoes
2 medium-sized onions
25-30 fresh young vine leaves (or 1 tin)
1 tablespoonful of lemon juice
4 tablespoonsful of olive oil
Salt and pepper

350°F (177°C/Gas Mark 4)

Cook the brown rice, wash the courgettes and chop finely. Peel and chop the onions and chop up the tomatoes, reserving the juice. Heat up the olive oil and add the chopped onions and the courgettes.

Sauté until the courgettes are tender and then add the tomatoes, the lemon juice and the seasonings. Mix together with the cooked brown rice. This is the filling for the dolmades.

Place a spoonful of the filling in each vine leaf and roll them up tightly, folding the sides in carefully to avoid spillage. Place a lining of vine leaves in a baking dish and arrange the dolmades in it, packed closely together. Pour the reserved tomato juice (or some water) over them, cover and bake for 20 minutes. Serve hot.

Cabbage leaves can be used if vine leaves are hard to come by (see also Stuffed Cabbage Leaves, p. 110).

Brown Rice, Cheese and Leeks

2 medium-sized leeks
1 large onion
1 oz. (25g) of margarine
4 oz. (100g) of grated cheddar cheese
1 tablespoonful of cream or top of the milk
Black pepper and sea salt
1 cupful of brown rice
Chopped parsley to garnish

Bring 2 cupsful of water and a little sea salt to the boil. Add the brown rice, cover tightly and simmer on a very low heat for 50 minutes. Meanwhile, *sauté* the onion and the leeks in the margarine until they are cooked but not brown.

Place the cooked rice in a warm serving dish, add the *sautéed* onion and leeks, the cream (or top of the milk), the grated cheese and the seasonings to taste. Place in a warm oven for 5-10 minutes so that the cheese is thoroughly melted. Garnish with parsley before serving.

This makes a light but extremely filling evening meal.

Sweetcorn Soufflé

1 small tin of sweetcorn
2 oz. (50g) of margarine
½ pt. (275ml) of milk
2 tablespoonsful of 81% stoneground flour
3 egg yolks
4 egg whites
Salt and pepper
Paprika

350-375°F (177-191°C/Gas Mark 4)

Cook and drain the sweetcorn. In a medium-sized saucepan, melt the margarine and add the flour to form a *roux*. Remove from the heat and gradually add the milk. Season with the salt, pepper and paprika. Return to the heat and cook gently, stirring constantly.

Allow to cool and then add the sweetcorn. Mix in well and add 3 well-beaten egg yolks followed by 4 egg whites that have been whisked until stiff. Fold in well and turn the mixture into a well-greased *soufflé* dish. Bake for 35-40 minutes until well risen.

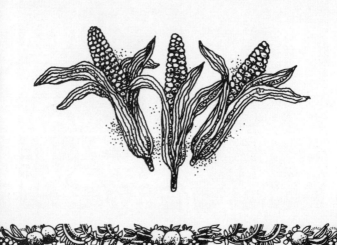

POTATOES, CHEESE AND EGGS

Here are a few ideas for using up these common but nutritious items. They can be used for quick and easy lunches and also as the basis for more substantial evening meals, filled out with accompanying vegetables and perhaps home-made soup to begin with.

Potatoes Romanov

6 large potatoes
1 carton of cottage cheese
4 oz. (100g) of cheddar cheese
3 spring onions
½ pt. (275ml) of sour cream
1 clove of garlic
Salt
Paprika

350°F (177°C/Gas Mark 4)

Peel the potatoes and boil them. Then cut them up into small neat cubes. Mix the cottage cheese, the garlic clove (chopped finely), spring onions, salt (to taste) and the sour cream and combine with the potatoes. Place the mixture in a well-greased casserole and sprinkle the top with the grated cheddar cheese.

Top with paprika and bake for about ½ hour.

Potato Cakes

6 oz. (175g) of mashed potatoes
8 oz. (225g) self-raising flour
3 oz. (75g) margarine
¼ cupful of milk
1 teaspoonful of salt
Caraway seeds (optional)

400°F (204°C/Gas Mark 6)

Mix the flour, salt and margarine and add the mashed potato and enough milk to form a soft dough. Roll on to a floured board to about ½-⅓ of an inch thick and cut into ten or twelve rounds with a 3-inch cutter.

The caraway seeds can be sprinkled on the top if desired. Bake the cakes on a greased baking sheet for 20-30 minutes.

Eat the potato cakes split and spread with butter or margarine. They make an unusual and fortifying breakfast dish when served with mushrooms or grilled tomatoes — an excellent way of fighting the bacon-orientated fried breakfast. The dough can be prepared on the previous night ready for the morning.

Hot Cheesy Potatoes

6 large potatoes
8 oz. (225g) of cottage cheese
½ pt. (275ml) of single cream
2 cloves of garlic (pressed or finely chopped)
3 spring onions (finely chopped)
1 teaspoonful of salt
4 oz. (100g) of grated cheddar cheese
Paprika

350°F (177°C/Gas Mark 3)

Boil the potatoes until they are just tender and cut into small cubes. Combine the cream, cottage cheese, salt, and spring onions with the potatoes.

Put the mixture into a buttered ovenproof dish and sprinkle grated cheese and a little paprika over the top. Bake for about ½ hour and serve hot.

Potato and Cheese Layers

2 lb (900g) of medium to large potatoes
4 oz. (100g) of grated cheese
2 large onions
Margarine
Pepper
Salt
A little top milk

375°F (191°C/Gas Mark 5)

Peel the potatoes and boil them until they are almost cooked. Meanwhile, prepare a large, flat ovenproof dish and peel and slice the onions thinly.

Drain the potatoes and slice them thinly. Cover the base of the dish with them and sprinkle with grated cheese and the onions. Dot with margarine, salt and pepper and cover with another layer of potatoes and onions. Repeat until the dish is full, finishing with a layer of potatoes.

Pour a little top milk over the top so that it trickles down between the layers. Dot generously with margarine, salt and pepper and bake for 30 minutes or until the potatoes begin to brown.

Easy Oven Omelette

4 eggs (free-range)
4 oz. (100g) of grated cheese
1 small onion
1 tomato
6 medium-sized mushrooms
A few peas
Salt
Pepper
1 oz. (25g) of margarine

350°F (177°C/Gas Mark 4)

Heat the oven. Place the margarine in a 7-inch *soufflé* dish and place in the oven to melt. Chop the onions, tomatoes and mushrooms and add these to the dish. Leave to cook for a few minutes.

Whisk the eggs, add the cheese and the seasonings, and pour carefully into the *soufflé* dish. Cook for about 20 minutes until it is well risen and brown.

Spinach and Egg

½ lb (225g) of chopped spinach
2 oz. (50g) of margarine
8 oz. (225g) of cottage cheese
3 eggs (beaten)
¼ pt. (150ml) of double cream
Parmesan cheese (grated)
Salt
Pepper

375°F (191°C/Gas Mark 5)

Cook the spinach and drain well. Season and add the margarine. Then add the cottage cheese, the parmesan, the cream and the beaten eggs. Mix thoroughly.

Spread the mixture in a blind cooked flan case and bake for about 40 minutes.

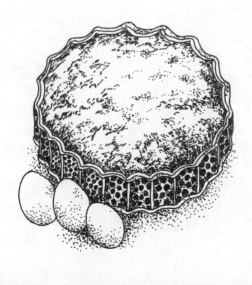

Oeufs Florentine

1 packet (8 oz./225g) of frozen leaf or chopped spinach, *or*
8 oz. (225g) of fresh spinach
2 eggs
¼ pt. (150ml) of thick cheese sauce
1 dessertspoonful of single cream
12 oz. (350g) of grated cheese
Small knob of margarine
Salt and pepper

375°F (191°C/Gas Mark 5)

Cook the fresh or the frozen spinach and spread on the bottom of an ovenproof dish. Make two small wells in the centre and crack an egg into each. Spoon the cheese sauce over the mixture and sprinkle with grated cheese.

Place in the oven and cook until the eggs are set (test them by just gently moving aside the sauce with a knife). Place under a hot grill to brown.

Baked Cheese Eggs

4 oz. (100g) of cheddar cheese
4 eggs
1 oz. (25g) of margarine
4 tablespoonsful of cream or top of the milk
Salt
Pepper

425°F (218°C/Gas Mark 6)

Grate 2 oz. (50g) of the cheese and slice the remainder very thinly. Grease an ovenproof dish well with the margarine. Cover the base of the dish with the cheese slices. Break the eggs over the slices, taking care not to disturb the yolks. Season with salt and pepper and then pour the cream or the top of the milk over the eggs. Finally, sprinkle with the grated cheese.

Bake for 15 minutes and then brown under the grill.

Cheese Soufflé

4 oz. (100g) of grated cheddar cheese
2 oz. (50g) of margarine
1 oz. (25g) of 81% plain flour
½ level teaspoonful of salt
¼ level teaspoonful of Cayenne pepper
1 teaspoonful of mustard
3 large eggs

380°F (195°C/Gas Mark 5)

Make a *roux* by melting the margarine then adding the flour and the seasonings gradually. Add the milk, stirring all the time, to form a smooth sauce. Bring slowly to the boil and continue to cook for 1 minute. Set aside to cool.

Meanwhile, separate the eggs and beat the whites until they are stiff. Whisk the yolks into the sauce and then fold in the grated cheese. Using a metal spoon, gently fold the sauce into the egg whites and pour the mixture into a greased 7-inch *soufflé* dish.

Bake in the centre of the oven for 40-45 minutes. Serve immediately.

Cheese Pudding

4 oz. (100g) of grated cheese
2 oz. (50g) of brown breadcrumbs
2 eggs
¾ pt. (425ml) milk (or milk with single cream)
1 teaspoonful of dried mustard
Salt and pepper

350°F (177°C/Gas Mark 3)

Mix the breadcrumbs, cheese and seasonings lightly together. Beat the eggs and milk together, then strain into the breadcrumb mixture.

Combine the ingredients well and pour into a greased ovenproof dish. Bake for ¾ hour.

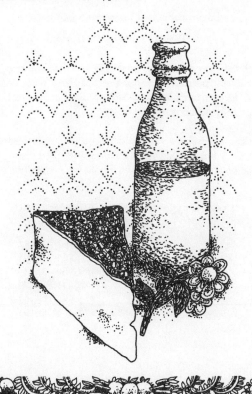

Savoury Cheesecake

Base:

**4 oz. (100g) of savoury crackers
1½ oz. (40g) of margarine**

Filling:

**12 oz. (350g) of grated cheddar cheese
2 eggs (separated)
5 tablespoonsful of single cream
3 oz. (75g) of margarine
2 tablespoonsful of chopped parsley
Salt
Pepper (Cayenne)
Dried mustard
Cucumber and parsley to garnish**

275-300°F (135-149°C/Gas Mark 1)

Crush the savoury crackers. Melt the margarine and add the crackers. Press the mixture into the base and sides of a 7-inch flan dish. Cream the 3 oz. (75g) of margarine and add the seasonings and parsley, then the egg yolks, cheese and cream, and mix thoroughly.

Whisk the egg whites and add to the mixture. Spoon into a flan dish and bake for about an hour or until firm. Garnish with slices of cucumber and parsley. Serve either hot or cold.

MISCELLANEOUS IDEAS

Finally, a mixed bag of recipes. To begin with there are some ideas for obvious 'meat substitute' meals — dishes that will strike a faint chord of recognition in a carnivore.

Basic Tomato Filling

This can be used as the basis for a number of dishes:

1 large onion
1 tablespoonful of olive oil
1 tin of tomatoes
1 small green pepper (or leeks, in season)
4 oz. (100g) of mushrooms
1 teaspoonful of sea salt
Ground black pepper
1 bay leaf
Pinch of mixed herbs
1 teaspoonful of tomato ketchup

Sauté the onion in the oil. Add the green pepper (or leeks) and *sauté* for a further few minutes. Add the tomatoes, chopping into lumps with kitchen scissors during cooking.

Add the seasonings and the tomato ketchup. Simmer for 15 minutes. Remove the bay leaf.

This filling can be used as the basis for the following:

Meatless Lasagne

350-400°F (176-204°C/Gas Mark 4-5)

Cook sufficient strips of pasta (wholemeal, if prefered) in boiling salted water to which 1 tablespoonful of oil has been added (this prevents the strips of pasta sticking together) for 15 minutes. Drain.

Grease a suitable ovenproof dish and lay one layer of cooked pasta in the bottom. Cover this with a layer of grated cheese and basic tomato filling followed by another layer of pasta, and so on until the dish is almost full. The last layer should be pasta.

Make a cheese sauce with ½ pt. (275ml) of milk and pour over the lasagne. Sprinkle with grated cheese and bake for 15-20 minutes until the top is brown.

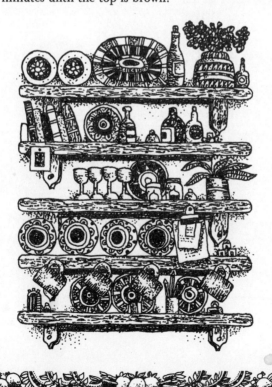

Rice Noodles or Spaghetti

Boil the required amount of pasta or rice in salted water.
Drain when *al dente*. Replace in the saucepan adding a
tablespoonful of margarine or vegetable oil. Serve with the
basic tomato filling and grated cheese.

Finally, try the basic tomato filling with this next recipe:

Meatless Potato Moussaka

350-400°F (176-204°C/Gas Mark 4-5)

Cook 4 or 5 medium-sized potatoes until they are almost done. Slice lengthways. Cover the bottom of a suitable greased ovenproof dish. Pour in the basic tomato filling so that the potatoes are covered. Lay another layer of potatoes over this followed by more filling, and so on, finishing with a layer of potatoes.

Make a basic cheese sauce using ½ pt. (275ml) of milk. Remove from the heat when cooked and add one whisked egg and a teaspoonful of grated nutmeg. Pour over the potatoes, sprinkle with grated cheese, and cook for 30 minutes in the oven.

Chinese-style Noodles

Noodles
Bean sprouts (lightly boiled or lightly fried)
6-8 oz. (175-225g) of white fish, cooked and flaked
1 large cupful of chopped onion
1 cupful of cooked peas
1 tablespoonful of soy sauce
Parsley and black pepper to garnish

250°F (121°C/Gas Mark ½)

Boil the noodles until they are tender. Combine all the ingredients in a large, flat ovenproof dish. Warm through for 10-15 minutes in the oven.

Garnish with parsley and serve with crisply-cooked cabbage or with green beans tossed in black pepper and margarine (or butter).

Stuffed Pancakes

Batter:

4 oz. (100g) of 81% stoneground flour
1 egg
½ pt. (275ml) of milk
Pinch of salt

Filling:

2 oz. (50g) margarine
1 oz. (25g) 81% stoneground flour
6 oz. (175g) of grated cheddar cheese
2 oz. (50g) of sliced button mushrooms
1 small onion
Salt and pepper
Vegetable oil for frying

Sieve the 4 oz. (100g) of flour and the salt into a basin. Beat the egg and the milk into the centre gradually until the batter is smooth. Allow to stand.

Meanwhile, make the filling by frying the mushrooms and the onion gently in the margarine. Remove the mushrooms and onion and add the 1 oz. (25g) of flour to the melted margarine that remains. Gradually add the milk, stirring all the time, and cook for 1 minute. Remove from the heat and put back the mushrooms and onion, together with the grated cheese and the seasonings.

Use the batter to make eight thin pancakes in an 8-inch, heavy-based frying pan and keep them warm by placing them on a plate standing on a pan of hot water. Place a piece of greased greaseproof paper between each pancake. Place a tablespoonful of the filling onto each pancake, fold into four and arrange on a hot dish. Serve immediately.

Lasagne Rolls

8 lasagne sheets
1 tablespoonful of vegetable oil

Filling:

½ lb (225g) of chopped spinach
2 tablespoonsful of grated parmesan cheese
8 oz. (225g) of cottage cheese
Pinch of grated nutmeg
Salt and pepper

Sauce:

2 large onions
1 clove of garlic   + aubergine
2 tablespoonsful of vegetable or olive oil
14 oz. (400g) tin of tomatoes
1 teaspoonful of mixed herbs
2 tablespoonsful of tomato ketchup
4 oz. (100g) of grated cheddar cheese

350°F (177°C/Gas Mark 4)

Cook the lasagne in boiling water to which a tablespoonful of
oil and some salt has been added for 10 minutes. Drain and
separate the sheets and lay them on some kitchen paper.
Cook the spinach, drain well and add the cheeses, nutmeg,
salt and pepper, taking care to mix well. Divide the mixture
equally between the lasagne sheets, spread and roll up.
Arrange the rolls on end, packed closely together in a greased
ovenproof dish.

Make the sauce by peeling the onions and the garlic and
chopping them finely. *Sauté* them in the vegetable or olive
oil for about 5 minutes then add the tomatoes and the
tomato ketchup. Boil and then simmer for about 5 minutes.

Pour this sauce over the lasagne rolls, sprinkle with grated
cheese and cook for about an hour.

Brown Rice with Fish

3 cupsful of cooked brown rice
Any cooked fresh fish
1 medium-sized onion
2 tablespoonsful of single cream
1 tablespoonsful of margarine
½ cupful of cooked peas
½ clove of garlic, finely chopped
1 teaspoonful of mixed mustard
½ cupful of chopped parsley

This recipe is simplicity itself. Just combine all the ingredients in a warm ovenproof dish and cook in a medium oven for 5-10 minutes.

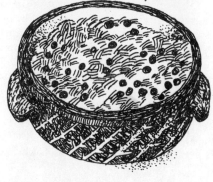

Tuna Fish Crumble

Sauce:

¼ pt. (150ml) of single cream combined with milk
1 oz. (25g) of 81% stoneground flour
1 oz. (25g) of margarine
1 teaspoonful of white wine
2 teaspoonsful of tomato ketchup
Pinch of salt
1 tin of tuna fish
Black pepper
Crushed garlic or garlic salt
1 teaspoonful of mixed mustard

Crumble:

6 oz. (175g) of wholemeal stoneground flour
3 oz. (75g) of margarine
1 teaspoonful of sea salt

350°F (176°C/Gas Mark 4)

Melt the margarine and the flour to form a *roux*. Gradually add milk and cook on a low heat for five minutes. Add seasonings.

Prepare the crumble topping by working the flour, margarine and salt with the fingers until it is the consistency of fine breadcrumbs. Drain the oil from the tin of tuna fish and flake. Combine with the sauce and pour into a greased ovenproof dish. Sprinkle with the crumble mixture and bake in the oven until the top is browned.

Serve either as a main course with a fresh salad or as a starter in small individual dishes.

Cheese Loaf

3 oz. (75g) of margarine
8 oz. (225g) of 81% self-raising flour
1 level teaspoonful of baking powder
1 level teaspoonful of dry mustard
½ level teaspoonful of salt
½ level teaspoonful of black pepper
¼ level teaspoonful of paprika
1 large onion
1 egg
3 oz. (75g) of strong cheese
8 tablespoonsful of milk

380°F (193°C/Gas Mark 5)

Chop the onion finely and fry in margarine until soft. Mix the dry ingredients together thoroughly in a large mixing bowl. Add the onion, egg and milk and beat well with a wooden spoon. Place the mixture in a 1 lb (450g) loaf tin that has been lined with greaseproof paper. Bake for 40-45 minutes.

Remove from the oven and leave in the tin to cool for about 5 minutes. Turn out the loaf, slice and spread with margarine or butter.

Try this and the next recipe if you are tired of the awful monotony of sandwiches in your lunchbox and to entice your carnivores away from the inevitable meat fillings.*

* For a host of original and ingenious suggestions for brightening up the lunchbox see *The Wholefood Lunchbox* by Janet Hunt (Thorsons, 1979).

Cheese Scones

2 oz. (50g) of margarine
8 oz. (225g) of 81% self-raising flour
¼ teaspoonful of salt
¼ teaspoonful of black pepper
½ teaspoonful of dry mustard
¼ teaspoonful of paprika
3 oz. (75g) of finely-grated strong cheese
1 teaspoonful of parmesan cheese
1 egg
5 tablespoonsful of milk

425°F (218°C/Gas Mark 6)

Put the margarine, strong cheese, parmesan, seasonings and flour into a mixing bowl and crumble with the finger tips to form fine breadcrumbs. Make a well in the centre and add the milk and the egg. Mix thoroughly with a wooden spoon and turn the mixture on to a lightly-floured board or a marble slab and roll out to ¾-inch thickness. Cut out into scone shapes and place on a greased baking tray. Brush the tops with milk and bake for 12-15 minutes.

As well as having them in a lunchbox with a salad these scones are perfect for a winter tea-time split and spread with butter or margarine.

Lemon and Orange Drink

2 oranges
2 lemons
2 lb (1kg) of granulated sugar
2¼ pt. (1¼ litres) of boiling water
1 oz. (25g) of tartaric acid

Squeeze the juice from the oranges and lemons and then roughly chop up the skins. Set the juice on one side. Dissolve the sugar and the tartaric acid in the boiling water and add the peel. Leave to stand until cool (about 20 minutes) and then add the juice. Cover and leave to stand for about 6 hours. It is a good idea to make the drink in the evening and allow it to stand overnight.

Strain and then bottle. Dilute to taste and be sure to keep it refrigerated. This is a perfect additive-free thirst-quencher for a long hot summer afternoon and it is also much appreciated coming cold and tangy from a flask in a stuffy office.

Salad Nicoise

Finally, because no vegetarian cookbook should be without one, a salad. There are so many salads and you really can let your imagination run riot in creating them. But this is a quick and easy one, ideal for a rushed summer supper.

2 lettuce hearts
1 tin of tuna fish
4 oz. (100g) of cooked green beans
12 black olives
1 medium-sized onion, peeled and sliced in rings
2 tomatoes, cut in wedges
1 green pepper (sliced)
1 hard-boiled egg, cut into 4 wedges

Dressing:

4 fl. oz. (100ml) of olive oil
2 fl. oz. (50ml) of white wine or cider vinegar
Pinch of mixed herbs
1 clove of garlic (crushed)
1 teaspoonful of brown sugar
½ teaspoonful of dry mustard

Wash and dry the lettuce, tear into bite-sized pieces and arrange on a large serving plate. Drain the oil from the tuna fish and mash the fish gently. Form into a mound in the centre of the serving plate and arrange the tomatoes, onion, egg, olives and beans around the fish.

Make the dressing by mixing the oil, vinegar or white wine, herbs, garlic, sugar and mustard in a screwtop jar. Shake well. Pour the dressing over the salad and serve immediately with crusty brown bread.

When you think the time is right (and only you can judge the right moment) try a few of these recipes out on your meat eaters. Don't forget to get their comments and if they genuinely do not like something try and stop yourself from abusing their depraved taste. If, on the other hand, all goes well, try introducing one or two completely vegetarian menus a week: for instance, try replacing the traditional British Sunday lunch with a starter of melon and grapefruit, followed by nut roast and non-meat gravy, batter puddings, roast potatoes, brussels sprouts or broccoli and carrots. Or, for a light but filling supper, try chilled carrot soup, stuffed cabbage leaves, baked potatoes in their jackets filled with grated cheese and a mixed green salad.

Above all, remember to be satisfied with small victories. Once the taste for non-meat food has been established, the rest may be easier than you think.

AFTERWORD

I have my doubts . . . whether a sound enjoyment of animal
food can develop itself freely in any human subject who is
always in torment from tight boots.

Charles Dickens, *David Copperfield*, xxviii

The subversion of carnivores, as I hope this book has indicated, is
not a dark and despicable activity. There is nothing immoral or
desperately underhand about it. Its main features are discretion
and a good deal of patience and it is, above all, an attitude, a
state of mind, rather than a narrow set of rules; a belief, not just
in the cause itself, but in your own capacity to justify with hard
facts and practical demonstration what may be only an intense but
inarticulate emotional commitment. It assumes, naturally, a moral
stance, but it is not inflexibly didactic; and it respects the rights of
others to differ — provided, of course, that their dissent is also
based on an objective appraisal of all the facts.

Your willingness to listen as well as talk, and to argue, not with
passion alone, but with knowledge, restraint and courtesy, are
inestimable strengths. Combined with the gradual introduction of a
few vegetarian meals a week, or even complete vegetarian menus,
you may find that your meat eaters, as I did, suddenly realize that
vegetarianism is a viable and acceptable alternative.

The problem is that carnivores generally react on prejudice, not
on a clear appreciation of the vegetarian alternative. Indeed, for
many meat eaters the vegetarian alternative is a misty, crank-
haunted land peopled with sentimental eccentrics. Their understanding of what living without meat really means in practice is
sadly defective — and so is their knowledge of what animals have
to suffer to sustain a carnivorous population.

But, like David Copperfield's 'tight boots', the continual pricking of the carnivorous conscience by the vigilant subversive vegetarian and the seizing of every opportunity to prove that blood and bone are not essential for good eating may eventually break the spell and finally dissipate the inherited dependence on the corpses of our fellow-creatures.

USEFUL ADDRESSES

Animal Advocates
92 Fleet Street
LONDON EC4

Compassion in World Farming
Lyndum House
PETERSFIELD
Hampshire

National Anti-Vivisection Society (NAVS)
51 Harley Street
LONDON W1N 1DD

National Petition for the Protection of Animals
60 Wellington Road
CROWTHORNE
Berkshire RG11 7LD

The British Union for the Abolition of Vivisection
47 Whitehall
LONDON SW1

The General Election Co-ordinating Committee for Animal
Protection (GEECAP)
10 Queensferry Street
EDINBURGH EH2 4PG

The Vegetarian Centre and Bookshop
53 Marloes Road
Kensington
LONDON W8 6LA

The Vegetarian Society (UK) Ltd.
Parkdale
Dunham Road
ALTRINCHAM
Cheshire WA14 4QG

LIST OF RECIPES